Honor comes Hard

Writings from the
California Prison
System's Honor Yard

edited by
Luis J. Rodriguez and
Lucinda Thomas

Tia Chucha Press
Los Angeles

Printed in the United States.

ISBN-13 978-1-882688-38-8

Book Design: Jane Brunette

Cover painting: "Freedom," 24" x 30", by Kitrona Paepule, a Samoan American currently serving a "life without possibility of parole" sentence.

PUBLISHED BY:

Tia Chucha Press
A project of Tia Chucha's Centro Cultural
PO Box 328
San Fernando, CA 91341
www.tiachucha.com

DISTRIBUTED BY:

Northwestern University Press
Chicago Distribution Center
11030 South Langley Avenue
Chicago IL 60628

Tia Chucha Press is the publishing wing of Tia Chucha's Centro Cultural, Inc., a 501 (c) 3 nonprofit corporation. Tia Chucha's Centro Cultural has received funding from the National Endowment for the Arts, the California Arts Council, Los Angeles County Arts Commission, Los Angeles Department of Cultural Affairs, The California Community Foundation, the Annenberg Foundation, Thrill Hill Foundation, the Middleton Foundation, Not Just Us Foundation, among others, as well as donations from Bruce Springsteen, John Densmore, Lou Adler, Richard Foos, Adrienne Rich, Tom Hayden, Dave Marsh, Mel Gilman, Jack Kornfield, Jesus Trevino, David Sandoval, Denise Chávez and John Randall of the Border Book Festival, Luis & Trini Rodríguez, and more.

CONTENTS

INTRODUCTION: "A CHANCE TO LIVE LIKE HUMAN BEINGS"

PRISON WRITING has a long and illustrious history in the United States—home of the modern correctional system, and currently the world's largest jailer: In the first decade of the 21st century, this country garnered the distinction of having more prisoners per capita than any other nation in the world. We need to have access to the incarcerated writings of incarcerated men and women.

The largest state prison system is in California. By this writing there were around 155,000 people behind bars in 33 facilities—another 8,000 had been released into various alternative sentencing programs, like home monitoring, and another 6,000 were farmed out to other states. Yet the only Honor Yard in the state's Department of Corrections was at the California State Prison, Los Angeles County, in Lancaster, CA. These are the men that despite often horrendous crimes—many are lifers, with a few going on three decades behind bars—have proven their capacity to dream, to create, to write, to change.

In December of 2007, I entered the A-Unit—a maximum-security section of the prison where the Honor Yard was housed—as a writer/educator through the prison's arts education program run by Lucinda Thomas. Here music, art, theater, writing, and sports were offered on a regular basis to men who agreed to stay drug and violence free, and who agreed to the discipline of the various arts disciplines to bring positive and worthwhile goals to their prison existence. In the workshops I facilitated, I worked with highly-engaged poets, novelists, essayists, playwrights, screenwriters, and short story writers for around eight months, most every Sunday, eight hours a day.

This book is a result of that workshop, although it also includes writings done before and since, and even from those who did not participate. Some of the men are no longer in A-Unit. A couple of the participants have since been released.

The history of the Honor Yard goes back to the winter of 2000 when prisoner Kenneth E. Hartman proposed a plan to house together Level IV inmates who were tired of the prison yard politics. Then-Warden Ernie Roe and a priest named Thomas White began a volunteer program with some 600 men of all races and communities. It proved to be quite a success. One 2003 prison-sanctioned study found that weapons infractions fell by 88 percent; violence and threatening behavior dropped by 85 percent; and drug-related offenses were down by 43 percent. In addition, the Honor Yard for five years held the record as the most violence free of all state prison yards.

Unfortunately, as the prison population outgrew the existing facilities statewide, the Lancaster prison became a reception facility and the program had to be closed.

Public outcry and support from people such as State Senator Gloria Romero helped create the "Honor Yard Bill" in 2006, established by the Public Safety Commission. The bill passed through the state legislature, but Governor Arnold Schwarzenegger failed to sign it. As Lucinda Thomas wrote, "not vetoed, unsigned, with the directive that [the Governor] was not going to legislate a classification that should be implemented administratively... this began the slow but steady infiltration of knuckleheads bent on returning to the convict politics of drug use and segregation. The population of the Honor Yard has been compromised to barely one third that meet the criteria."

To add, Lucinda writes:

There is a silence on the Honor Yard now, a confusing tone that floats among the men. Although there has been a formal recognition of the honor program criteria direct from Secretary of Corrections Matthew Kate earlier in 2009, it perhaps came too little, too late. With the bottom falling out of the economy, almost all of the programming is being stripped from the Department of Corrections, effective January 2010. A full two-thirds of education staff have been laid off including Arts In Corrections, Vocations, and Coastline College courses. Okay, now what? Will the Progressive Programming Yard (Sacramento eventually changed the Honor Yard name, one they despised) dissolve into old school convict politics with nothing to do? Or can they implement the solution of bringing in volunteers off the street? This is a tricky model at best, as any volunteer will attest to. It is very disheartening to help out in a place where you are treated like an inmate. As the Institution Artist Facilitator within Arts In Corrections, we have had 25 years experience in utilizing volunteers and contractors. We worked well within the system, gently guiding volunteers through the complicated structure of custody. We have also had inmates teaching other inmates for years as it affects change within the teacher and within the man taught.

A few months ago I requested a young prisoner, 20 years old, be assigned to me. He had come from Youth Authority, there since 14, where his allegiance to race was foremost. Slowly he learned tolerance for another's expression and a pride in himself as an artist and a man with his identity residing in the best of his race. If he transfers to another yard he will be hurt or worse for tolerating others. Whose responsibility is this young man's fate? He will be getting out in five years and if the strength of his independence isn't continued, society will suffer. Well, all you high on "tough on crime and sentencing" may say that he made his choice at 14 and is now being punished. But if programming is stopped, it's we who will be punished. The hard knock prison life has proven not only to be an unsuccessful deterrent—it is college for predator gangster behavior. With the average cost of housing an inmate at $48,000 a year, all the system would have to do would be to release one non-violent parole violator to pay my salary. A parole violator, of which there are 26,000, is someone who neglects to check in with their probation officer or gives a dirty urine analysis.

If the legislators do not intervene and Arts In Corrections is dissolved after 25 years of rehabilitative programming, you can rest assured I and the other Artist Facilitators will volunteer as our other commitments allow.

Never give up, never stand by.

AROUND THE TIME of that writing, in October of this year, Lucinda Thomas wrote to say she received a lay-off notice along with other Arts In Corrections personnel. I want to thank Ms. Thomas for bringing me into the prison and helping me put together this book. She did the bulk of the work of gathering this material. I also want to thank Dave Mashore of the Catalyst Foundation for trying to get more writings. Thanks also to prisoner Irving Relova and volunteer Julie Harmon Chavez for assisting in this. And to workshop participant Hugo Machuca for keeping hope alive (after 28 years behind bars, Hugo was finally released in the summer of 2009). And a big thanks to Jane Brunette for the design of this book, but also for her help in editing.

In particular I want to give a special thanks to Kenneth E. Hartman, who despite a life sentence for murder close to thirty years ago, has become a leader in prison reform by attempting to bring about the first arts-based honor yard in the California prison system. Mr. Hartman is also a widely published writer who in late 2009 came out with his first book, "Mother California: A Story of Redemption Behind Bars" (Atlas & Co).

So read this book in your hand and enjoy—there are many truths here. As Ms. Williams wrote, "these writings are testament to the bravery that if properly nurtured can change the face of corrections." And remember what Kenneth Hartman once told the *Los Angeles Times,* that the Honor Yard "is a chance to live like human beings."

—*Luis J. Rodriguez*
Winter 2009

DARREN L. ROBINSON

COVERED IN BLUE

It can be a warm, happy, sunny day.
The rays shining—warming your skin.
It's about floating on your back,
Drifting on daydreams, squinting your eyes against the bright.

It could be curling up, huddling under
That threadbare blanket, warming your toes.
It's that day when you no longer want to be you—
The day you wish never happened.
It's the eyes that see not only you;
They see in you. Holding. Piercing.
The day your oldest jeans become youth's comfortable disguise.
I have been covered in blue.
What about you?

DARREN L. ROBINSON

WHERE HAVE I BEEN?

I've been here, not there—
still inside the justice cage. Counted calendars,
waved goodbye to holidays. It's the same for all of us.

Stripped naked in front of God and all for
something I've never done. Seen friends far and wide rushed
    like a bum.

I've been face down in the mud while it rains.
awaiting another's ignorance.
Stood in line for twenty years
and it still doesn't make any sense.

Maimed and divorced in due course.
Played basketball, softball.
Still denied in the courts.

I've gone to trial.
Sentenced to life
to suffer. But only because I let down my family—
mainly my mother.

D.M. CROOKES

LOVE SPEAKS IN A
DIFFERENT LANGUAGE

I.
Crowded streets of broken backs are singing songs
to a needle at 6 a.m.
Eternal horror always comes with some blood,
pushing the past's pain into the heavens.
A man yelling "tokens for sale, tokens for sale."
Fifth and Broadway is hopping, and it feels like
I am in another country.

I love it down here, cute Mexican girls selling
fruit on one corner, on the opposite corner the
pain reliever.
Walking down Broadway is like being at an amusement park.
Every face.
Every emotion.
Every smell, including the stench of the rotten pit
from down below.

Hotels are home, where you're on a first name basis
with the roaches.
Huntington is home now, Rosslyn threw me out on my
ass, sat there on the curb of misery for about an hour,
shoving tar up my fucking nose.
You can find me in the hole strummin' the strat, and
always planning a scam in order to pay for this hole.

I will beep Fredo around 5 p.m., he will drop off presents
since his wife is convinced I am too skinny, she

sometimes brings me tamales; she wants to jump my bones.
Fredo will kill me, though. For now I will settle for
uptown and tamales.
          Love speaks in a different language.

II.

Sleep is overrated—going four or five days is normal.
Getting bored with the look, cut the T, and wash the
scalp with blue/black.
Girls always knocking on the door, asking for condoms
to fulfill hidden dreams.
Hookers from the underground, rejoice!!!
One reminds me of a famous actress, secretly I want
to bring her to a better world, but she has the mark
of the man that holds her domain on her leg.

Maids hold down forts, so I leave my door open to see
if they will try to rip me off; one bites, so I get to know her.
She's a lesbian; her girl is also a maid; we fool
around once in a while, but her love is for the same kind.
Nick's girl comes by often, in search of a doctor.
She's a breath of fresh air, a mass communicator,
also an ass seller, a shaker of many faces.
It's too bad her life falls short from the mud I was
trying to keep her from.
          Love speaks in a different language.

III.

Night time is paranoia, take the rail to the Frolic,
always enjoyed the old 45s.
Drinks flow like fireballs from a volcano, like a
woman swimming in a pool, like a junkie's rig into butter.

Girl behind the counter always got a smile, people
always welcome, it says.

Taylor makes her way back to the hole around 10 pm
every two to three days, she strips for the animals—
elephants throw peanuts at her.
She deserves better; she's a princess; she's a
goddess; she's a woman.
Instead, we lie to each other every night. She says:
"Gonna get clean in the morning, honey." I say:
"Me too, babe, me too."

Discovering holes in the world every night, my new
place is the taco shack on Broadway. I think I am
the gringo crazy enough to be there at 3 am. It's always
packed with grazers from a different world.
Tacos and horchata are so good, the only thing that
could keep me from them is prison.
Hot mamacitas strolling the line, cowboys in tow.
Loving it here, but . . .
Love speaks in a different language.

IV.
Making sure I always curl up with Taylor in the
early morning, reassuring ourselves of the deed ahead.
Sleep comes to her in my arms, to me it comes in
the form of a pass out.
Sparks fly from my cigarette outside the window,
waiting for the bakery to open up, coffee and pastry
for a buck.
Starting a new day is easy, especially when you
do not know what day it is.

Light from the morning jelly bean soothes the bones.
Grin from the woman behind the counter always
brings some conversation; a picture comes in the
mix. At least once a week she tries to hook me
up with her daughter—hot little mamacita—and mom
is a hot shit, got me laughing all the time, makes
my dark mornings light.

If she only knew: the great pretender, the great
scam artist, good clothes, good manners, good heart,
but underneath enough tracks to put Union Pacific
out of business.

Still I love it here, or do I? What is love and has
anybody ever really loved me?
        Will I ever be loved?
        Will I ever walk the aisle?
        Will I ever see a birth?
        Will I see a son play little league?
        Will I see a daughter go to the prom?
        Will I curl up with a better half forever?
            Because, right now,

    Love speaks in a different language.

D.M. CROOKES

CONFUSION OF THE DAYS

Festival of screeching fingernails
fall upon the naked souls of the wicked.

Ghosts of the past screaming at me through
a silencing metal door.
Chained to the moldy surface,
bellowing the urine stench of madness.

Mirage-filled deserts are the only
dreams of the future.
Concrete blocks are counted in twos;
dripping water is your best friend.

Confusion of the days is not far away—
years in the now become terror-filled.

Nothing is seen beyond the boundary—
only hate, misfortune and the coldness of the free.
Tears of pain flow through sockets of
hollow eyes.

Tomorrow makes no difference;
nightmares every day does not change the time.
Wishing for it to stop spinning
only brings massive loneliness.

A box the size of a small bathroom is home;
my companion is insanity.

D.M. CROOKES

CELL BLOCK SLUG

Misery falls from the mouth,
slicking through the hands of a clock.

Desperation of the few who care.

A world in a box secures the poor—
thousands of junkies stand still at the edge
as they sail across the tunnel of blood.

Crooked trees hang from the wire;
ravens use them for their nests.

Whispers of insanity
clear the madness from the herd.

Fighting the urge to medicate oneself
is only for the few who are chosen.

Growing old in places of despair,
fills the heart with concrete.

Screaming in the minds of the sorrow;
deaf silence in the arms of the free.

Fantasy of the opposite is here,
casting shadows across the desolate desert.

WEARING BLUE IS NOT COMFORTING.

D. M. CROOKES

MANDATORY

"HEY MANDATORY yard." Hey mandatory workout." I remember hearing this from time to time, as this is my second term in a California prison. I'm from back east, and also did some time back there. It was different—a lot different, although if my friends from back east were in trouble and they needed me on the yard, I would be there. That was a big change from mandatory yard: "We want you to bring this to the yard with you." The only time I heard that back east is when there was some kind of protest against the guards, warden, or the system in general.

During my first term out here, I was introduced to the hatred between the different races and I fell into this system of thinking. Even some of the guards have this mentality out here. It's a shame, when I think about it, the way it changed me. You see, when I was younger, a teenager I should say, I played a lot of sports: baseball, basketball, and football. So I had a lot of friends of all colors. The way I started thinking disturbed me sometimes.

When I hit prison for reception on my current term, I had been hating everybody, even some people from my own race. I had changed in a big way. That is when I heard for the first time, "Mandatory workout." Most of the people at this reception yard were parole violators. Other guys were waiting to get classified, some were classified and they were waiting on their transfers to other prisons. I had come from L.A. County where the racial tension was also very high. Keeping out of trouble was almost impossible, but I did it. I worked out a lot, so when I heard mandatory workout, I was very enthusiastic about it.

Not only was I happy with the workout, my roommate—or my cell mate—turned out to be a good guy and also liked the workout we did. During these workouts, one cell would call out what you should do, and then the rest of the cells would call out the numbers in the reps you were doing. Even though the other races had more people than we did, we were just as loud, and me and my cell mate were the loudest. So it was no surprise to us that when the men who called out the workout got their transfers, they asked us to replace them. A few weeks later, someone came and asked me if I wanted to work in the kitchen. He told me there was three of each race and they were short a white guy. Of course, the thought of getting out of the cell every day was intriguing, so I agreed.

We were allowed to go in the yard every other day and of course it was mandatory. There were so many incidents during our yard time that most of the time was spent on the ground. They had more alarms in this prison than any other prison I have been in. Race riots, the slashings and beatings of snitches and child molesters who would mysteriously hit the main line instead of being put in protective custody.

In the early morning the guards would let me out to go to work and after I served breakfast, I would take a break and join the workout in the block. That was when I would see the other guys working out in their cells. I thought everybody liked it until I saw them struggling with it. You see, most of these men just came off the streets, and they had not worked out in a while. The word mandatory was starting to get to me.

Around the same time, I was called to the counselor to get classified. The counselor was a black man, and he seemed like a nice guy, so we had a good conversation for about an hour. I noticed a radio in his office was playing, and it had been a few months since I had heard one. I said, "Man that sounds funky, who is that?" He smiled and told me who it was, then said I would be going to a level four prison because I had too much time. We talked for a little while longer, then I shook his hand and left.

A few weeks had gone by. The cell block had been interesting over that period. There had been a Mexicans-against-the-Blacks riot, three Mexicans had slashed and beat another Mexican in the chow hall, and a white guy had been forced into protective custody for being in a gang he was not supposed to be in. I was getting tired of being at that prison and was hoping my transfer would come soon.

Then one day I was called back to the counselor's office. He sat me down and told me he had just gotten off the phone with a counselor at a prison in Lancaster. The counselor at Lancaster had told him about a new yard they where putting together called an honor yard: a place where there were no politics and that had programming. When they asked him if he had anyone who met the criteria, he said he thought of me, and then he asked me if I was willing to give this place a try. I thought about it, then I told him all right, I'll give it a shot. It's not definite, he said, you still have to go through classification when you get there.

Now I always get nervous when I am moving to a new prison. It's the fear of the unknown, I guess. When I got there they put me on orientation row, and to my relief, one of the guys on the bus was my cell mate.

To me it seemed the same at first, considering the prison had been on lock down. When the prison got off lock down a week or so later, I realized I was somewhere different. No one had came by to tell me there was mandatory yard or workout.

About thirty days later, I was classified, and was accepted to the honor yard program. Soon after that I was moved to the main line, and I found out how small the world is. Someone came up to me and said, Do I know you from somewhere? We soon figured out we had done time in the same prison back east. We got to know each other, and he became a good friend, and of course, my new workout partner.

It was nice to be able to workout when I wanted to, and when they called yard and opened my door for it, I could stay in if I wanted. This is when I started drawing. When I was back in school, art was the one class I showed up for. Even though I did not pursue it back then, I thought it would be great if I could teach myself how to draw. It turned out to be a great time killer also.

A few months down the road, someone asked me if I played sports. A couple weeks later I joined a softball team. I had not played sports in prison since the summer of 1988. What I could not believe was I actually did not fear someone of another race having a bat in his hand. After that first year, I knew I made the right choice by coming here.

Years went by, and I met someone who was interested in the same music I was into. One day he asked me to read some of his poems. I read them and told him I liked them. He asked me if I ever wrote any. Only a few, I said, and that was a long time ago. He got me to go to a workshop for writers. It was a good class. I have to admit, it surprised me when they said that they liked my poetry. I guess it did not hurt when I told them I was an amateur sky diver on the streets. We were so amateur that we jumped without chutes, I told them.

In addition to teaching myself how to draw, I bought some painting supplies so now I paint, draw, and write. Who would have thought? Don't get me wrong—it's still prison, and there are ups and downs. One of the downs was when my friend from back east had passed away. For about a year after, every time I worked out I pictured him standing there waiting. Like I said, this is still prison, and you take the good with the bad. Here there is more good than any prison yard I have been to.

The word mandatory is not a part of my life any more, but I think it should be. Once a month they should bus in women from other prisons and hold dances—that should be mandatory. And if any inmate tells me "It's mandatory, and you've got to do it," my answer would be: No thank you. I can think for myself and do what is right for me, and that's mandatory.

D.M. CROOKES

FIX ME

Morning time brings horns honking in succession
outside my window.
It's so loud my brain is in continuous parade mode.

Alison is flipping around the bed like a flounder.
She was smoking that shit last night.
Met her in a bar on the east side.
Seems like she's left a couple items every time
she comes over.
Pretty soon she will be living here.
Feel like kicking her out this morning, though—
just leave her to the madness.
I need to go visit my medicine cabinet.

Opening the door to the outside,
sunlight instantly gives me a headache.
Noise from the millions snap me back to reality.
Got to get to the subway.
I pass by a hot dog cart—
one where Dim got a dog,
then puked for two days.

Walking by the alleys:
sludge of the city has woken up to the stench of puke,
piss, shit and alcohol.
I walk the same walk every day.
It never fails—
I am wretching along with the rest of the animals.

My right foot is killing me:
starting to come out of the fog of the past couple nights,
I realize I have two left shoes on.

Sitting down in the corner of the subway,
there are some kids blasting rap music.
Some guys are sitting on the side of them—
look like they want to break the boom box.
I feel like I am in modern West Side Story.
Across from me sits a hot brunette in a mini skirt.
She's looking at my shoes.
The expression on her face sends us both into a
fit of laughter.

You think I would be embarassed,
but I am just caring about the fix.

GABRIEL RUBALCABA-CORRAL

WE DON'T NEED NO MORE TROUBLE

As I sit on this bench, or desk, I trip out because
I hear this music; it sounds so good to the ear,
the words, "We don't need no more trouble." It's true.
　Peace and love, what is that?
Peace, I think, is no more fighting.
And love, what is that? I can say I love you
but do I truly mean it? I would like to love.
Is love physical, or emotional? Or is it spiritual?

Trust. I don't know why but this word just
came up in my mind. What is trust?
I walk around this yard like I'm cold or
BAD, but I know somewhere deep down
I am not. I feel alone and abandoned.

THOMAS MICHAEL SIMMONS

NOEL, NOEL

IT WAS BACK in the fifties and sixties when Mom, Dad, Sis and I existed in this brick walkup on Chicago's South Side: three flats perched atop a photographer's studio, a clothing shop, and a laundromat. It must have been built at the turn of the century. The landlord was on one side, and a boozy widow on the other. Her son roamed the night with his golem—grunge long before it became a movement and proof that if you live long enough, you're bound to be typed and sorted. We were all linked by a rickety covered porch whose steps staggered down to a backyard that was the softball mecca for blocks around. Long lines stretched from worn pulleys over to another building, straining under the weight of drying clothes: a weird sort of semaphore spelling out to passersby what one was really like "underneath."

Across a side street was an old hardware store that held every bicycle known. A few blocks more and you had a family-run pizza place where the pies were handthrown, a theater boasting forty-five cent matinees, and a world-class comic book stand next to the Illinois Central tracks. Just a little further and you were dipping in Lake Michigan. Go in the opposite direction towards the sunset and you found a couple of novelty stores, and a burger joint where you could buy a bag of sliders for a buck. Across the street in front of us was one of the best and coolest barbers around. He'd jump on his Harley when the notion took him and ride down to Kentucky and back. Anything a city-kid could want—right?

Mom and Dad were really good Southern-folk who left for the city to grab whatever piece of the American Dream people of their generation understood. Without carping or whining —as only someone who loved his family could—Dad worked two jobs at textile mills across town. Mom had her hands full with all of us and also worked in the laundromat that she and Dad owned downstairs from us, all for that nice house with a big yard, a proper home. The dream would later become a two-story 1920's stucco: no white picket fence, but it did have a brown one.

Mingling hard work with the occasional pit-stop at bars and liquor stores, Dad wrestled with his own demons ... quietly, as those of his generation who had lived through the Second World War were raised to do. It wasn't until years—many years—later that I learned what some of these spectres were. While serving in the Pacific Fleet, a Kamikaze cut through the deck of a carrier he was on and he had saved some sailors, despite his own injuries. He didn't entertain fools or foolishness, born from the 25,000 volts that coursed through his body while as a lineman he tried to restore power to a hurricane-ravaged community while waist-deep in water. Someone sort of forgot to turn off a transformer — something that not only scarred his hands and body for the rest of his life, but his soul as well.

Mom was a Carolina-born farm girl he met when she worked as a telephone operator. She often felt alone, overwhelmed, and missed her family dearly. She felt like a fish out of water there in the city, and despite all the long treks to our grandparents, the calls, all the hugs and kisses and I-love-you's, just couldn't shake the melancholy. She and Dad would screw themselves up into these frenzied spats, spewing vile and hurtful things to each other and to us that neither really meant — so intense that the dogs would dart for shelter under a couch or bed, or in the solace of my sister's arms and mine. Dad would barge out the door, and she'd sulk, chain smoking her way through all that had happened, telling Sis and I that if it wasn't for us she wouldn't put up with any of it—your basic angst-sandwich wrapped in a lot of guilt.

Dad would stagger back, hours later, in some sort of stupor. The demons would surface to pin him to the floor, where I would sit, his head cradled in my lap, wiping his face and mouth with a cold wet rag as his ulcers rejected the day's binge as a foul-smelling brew of booze and bile into the small plastic pail I held between my knees. He'd lay there calling for Mom, who'd attempt to to come back and rail at him, only to retch herself at the sight and smell, then tear off to the bathroom to dry-heave it all away. Sis would be hiding in her room, crying through the closed door. And here I was, just a kid trying to figure out what to do, running back and forth, checking on all those I loved dearly, trying to convince them all that we loved each other and that things would get better.

There would be the blame games and threats screamed that one was going to leave the other. The day finally came when Dad reluctantly made good on his end, forty-some odd years later. Mom was there at his side as his eyes closed for the last time, both knowing that each was the love of the other's life. Mom followed him, two years later.

Such was life as I knew it for some time... except ...

There were good times ... magical times, when hope seemed more than real.

You see, I make these Christmas trees ...

THE FIRST TREE: I remember it was about a foot or so high, ceramic, and had these translucent "ornaments" of various hues inserted into tiny holes drilled into its boughs. They were lit from inside by a small bulb. It was placed inside a built-in glass, wood and mirrored hutch in our living room—the centerpiece of a carefully crafted holiday scene that Mom put together. You'd have a winter chalet, a small wax-candle Santa Claus and Frosty the Snowman, a ceramic Nativity scene, and Santa in his sleigh being pulled by assorted reindeer, all set amidst a snowfield of cotton-balls and angelhair. The glass and mirror fronts were covered in Christmas cards, stockings and aerosol snow, and framed by strings of multicolored twinkle lights.

As Sis and I got a little older, the folks upgraded to one of the-latest early 60s crazes: the six foot aluminum Christmas tree, replete with red, blue, green and silver glass ornaments, all washed by a floodlight with a rotating color wheel that was prone to soft buzzing. I reckon that's when I first knew I'd be a lighting director someday —something I must've imprinted.

Whether by fate or design, Thanksgiving and Christmas—especially Christmas—were the only times of the year that a detente of sorts was declared, and all were actually civil to one another. We'd go shopping with one parent for gifts that we could give the other, and visa-versa. There weren't any malls back then, but there were these large department stores, stories high. Once the folks thought to have me sit in Santa's lap, but that didn't quite go over too well. Let's just say from then on, the only communication to the jolly ol' Elf was via the mail.

Everything seemed to go right during those times of the year. Mom would busy herself decorating, and creating the feasts. There would be Thanksgiving turkey, Christmas ham, and Mom would make these incredible coconut cream cakes, pumpkin and sweet-potato pies that everyone wanted the recipes for. Holiday movies on the newly-acquired black and white console TV and holiday music from vinyl LPs; visits from various aunts, uncles, cousins, grandparents, and even the landlord and neighbors would supplant the boozy tirades, the stress, and loneliness that would generally be the norm. It was the one thing I always planned and hoped for, and looked forward to all year long. By the time New Year's Eve would arrive, it would all start to pass as if it were a dream. One would have to really beg to keep the tree and decor up through Epiphany, or at least until New Year's Day, just to keep the spirit alive a little longer —but I digress.

Anyway, Sis and I would help decorate over the years. Whether hanging cards and stockings, or devising various glitterati, responsibilities grew as we did. Finally the time would come... the tree! Obligatory branch-by-branch assemblage (often comedic, for lack of instructions) followed by careful placement of each ornament—but not until after scrupulous examination (and often as not, debate) was conducted from all angles.

After declaring all done, Mom would ask opinions, and like polite lil' bobbleheads, we nodded approval even if things seemed somewhat off. You see, she was prone to hanging everything imaginable out at the branch tips, leaving this bristly, multicolored pine cone of sorts shining proudly before us. But hey, Moms—especially "Christmas Moms"–are always right, right?

Remember those times you're caught off guard by that one question you'd better not answer too honestly? Coupled with a mother's innate, and legendary hyper-sensory perception that cuts through all smoke and mirrors, life's classic "uh-oh" moments are virtually guaranteed. Yours truly got nailed one morning while readying for school. There I was, looking somewhat morosely at our creation, when the dreaded "is anything wrong?" got asked, off-guard. Reflexive truth blurted out: "It seems empty inside." At that precise moment, all around me went into Sci-Fi slow motion for a few beats—Sis as she bopped in, the dogs, then stillness—by the look on Mom's face.

Walking with my Sis to school, her lack of animation gave insight into yet another universal truth: that all women, regardless of age or creed, are in fact part of some telepathic cabal that enables them to know instantly, without a word or sound uttered, what the other is feeling and thinking. It's a fact oblivious to the most testosterone-driven, but it seems cats are tuned into the link because as I walked by even they seemed to be shaking their heads as if to say, "Yeah, you really blew that one!"

Returning to climb the forty-odd creaking stairs up to the flat, I thought I could simply sneak past her as she was finishing up dinner at the stove. Just as I got near my room she called out, "Not so fast, mister." Caught. With a quiet smile she asked me to wash up and set the table for dinner. As I went through the flat to the bathroom, I passed where the tree stood, and something was changed. A closer inspection shown a remodeled affair aglow with ornaments inside and out! She spent all morning working on it, so it seemed. As we all sat down to eat, volumes of understanding were spoken with her wink.

Traditions. Some are good; some, well ... not so much, right? When not some mindless ritual based on some obscurity, or worse, "because it's always been done this way," they can be pretty cool, or rather, "warm and fuzzy." Heck, we all need to be more fuzzy if you asked me. Maybe you don't have any clue, but some traditions stay with you all your life. You wind up doing them, romancing them, simply because it feels right—no matter where or what, the memories take you back to that warmth, that sense of family and home, of hopes fulfilled.

There were two traditions born back then by our little clan, which forty-five or so years later are still clung to in one way or the other. The first was that all decorations, especially the tree, had to be up between Thanksgiving and the first of December—if at all possible before the classic stop-motion animated classic called "Rudolph the Red-Nosed Reindeer" was shown on television. That was the bellweather moment for all to be ready, along with some hot cocoa and popcorn!

The second was somewhat of a personal one with me though I hear that over the years it's been spreading. I don't know how I came up with it—just that one day when things seemed tense, I had the notion to pull a present out from under the tree, then slide on my back to where it was pulled from, and look up through the middle of the branches to see a wonderful mix of color and sparkle. With the music playing in the background, it was a small world of magic where I'd become lost. Lost, that is, until Mom's, "What are you doing?" startled me out from under it, scattering a few ornaments here and there in my wake. Embarrassed, I meekly said that I was just checking things out, and flitted off somewhere. One day though, I came back to find her laying there herself, gazing upward, hands folded on her belly. "You're right," came softly out from underneath. Then came the time when Dad would come home, and shake his head, laughing, at the three of us— Mom, Sis, and I—laying under the tree, presents scattered about us, displaced for the moment. My Sis still does this, I hear, to this day.

A YEAR CAME when in the early Spring, I was in my room reading a SpiderMan comic when the phone rang, followed by this incredible wail of grief that shook me to the bone. Sis and I ran quickly into the living room to find Mom collapsed on the sofa with Dad on the receiver. Grandpa wouldn't be coming that Christmas. When they went down to the funeral a few days later there was another call. Grandma wouldn't be coming, either. She passed three days after he from inconsolable grief. It was then I wished more than ever that our little tree was there to crawl under.

From that moment until the end of her days, Mom was filled with this unshakable melancholy. There would be the odd time or so when she seemed to rise out of it, only to eventually slide back into it again. Something had indeed profoundly changed her. Dad finally made enough to buy this really great 1920s stucco affair— two stories with a great looking marbled foyer with a high ceiling. That helped her a little, and that same year we upgraded to a seven-foot artificial Scotch Fir tree, which looked incredible. Yet even her smile belied this wistfulness, a sadness that clung like some parasite, sucking the joy from her very bones, it seemed. A little over a year later, Dad made the call for us to move down to Georgia, then back up to North Carolina so she would be nearer the aunts and uncles we loved. Maybe that would help somehow. He wanted desperately to do something to help—anything, as did we.

As Christmases came and went, it seemed that a little more of the joy and wonder that day once held was lost. A sadness seemed to etch away at all of us now. Sis decided one day to leave—she just couldn't bear it anymore—and stayed with some friends until she met a boyfriend that she would take up with, and eventually marry. This just added to the sense of loss, it seemed.

I stuck around for a few more years, trying hard to take care of whatever I could. I started doing work at a local Theater and Arts Center, working up to become a lighting director and designer, and occasional technical director. I had done quite a number of shows there, even a few barstar gigs for some big-named artists, and had a lot of publicity in the local papers. It was pretty good, except for the fact that neither Mom or Dad would come to any of the gigs—even after I won an award for a musical I designed. After I went pro, I was able at last to have them come up to see this Country Music tour I was on and meet some of their life-long idols. Dad especially liked it because he met some stars he once dreamed of performing with. That was cool.

Eventually, things drifted back to the morose, though. It finally came to the point where they no longer celebrated anything. Christmas just became another day to them. It seemed that it would fall on my Sis and I to keep the spirit alive, somehow. In the end, we all drifted apart from each other, no matter how hard we tried not to.

So here I was, off doing Rock tours, one-offs, and the like. It got to the point that the work I had been doing was noticed enough for me to be tapped to do some music videos and film work. People were looking for road techs to help suss out their productions, and it seemed I and a few others had gained a reputation for an innate ability to trouble-shoot problems and do gigs that others had thought impossible (or improbable, at least) to do. I started to rise slowly in the industry. I had even hooked up with a crew whose gaffer was doing a lot of productions, and who was an ex-road tech himself.

Yet, Mom, Dad, and Sis wouldn't be far from my mind, no matter where I would be in the world, or what I was doing. I worried for them. I'd call them often to see if they were okay, or if there was anything I could do. There would be the holiday or two that I'd show up and bring prezzies galore for all, yet have to fly out for another gig the next day. Such was life. Whether it was a hotel room or crew bus, I never had time to get a place of my own organized. It just didn't seem important then. Such was life. Hope did seem to rise from the cracks though, as Mom and Dad both seemed to be in better spirits. Though the tree remained packed away in storage, Mom took to making a small one of her own out of dried grape vines and ornaments that seemed popular with those who'd drop by to visit every so often.

Around the mid-to-late eighties, I had decided to help a group out with a 72-hour fashion marathon geared to raise money for the

AIDS ward at a local children's hospital when I bumped into this drop-dead gorgeous girl from New Zealand, and her family who were modeling their designs at the event. We hit it off right away — like peas and carrots— and started dating whenever and wherever we could. They seemed like the kind of family that you or anyone could hope to be a part of. New Zealanders, incidently, are big on holidays and family.

The year I met them, it turned out that they were in tough-straits financially. In trying to start up a boutique here in the States, her Dad had underestimated the costs, and they had been foolish in allowing themselves to be taken in and bilked for a good part of their money. They were living in this gloomy, cramped apartment a few blocks off the beach. Despite nearly losing everything they had, they still were filled with hope, and close to each other. So, without their asking (or even knowing, for the most part), I worked to help cover many of their needs. I was able to help their daughter give them their first Thanksgiving feast (she was a great cook!), and that year, I also found out that they hadn't celebrated Christmas for almost two years. The wheels up in the ol' melon started to turn...

You see, I make these Christmas trees ...

COMPLETELY UNAWARES, and off-guard, I asked my little kiwi if she wanted to go for a movie and dinner. She agreed, and off we went. But before dinner, we had a pit-stop at the local tree lot to pick up this fantastic looking fir tree with all the ornaments, bells and whistles you could imagine. We left with her station wagon loaded with gifts and the like, the tree strapped to its roof. We got to her place when her folks were asleep, and, like little Ninja-Elves, we shuttled everything upstairs, giggling. We worked through the night, full of cognac and chocolates, to have her folks awaken to a tree standing in full regalia before them, and one of the best Christmases they'd had in years. These are some of the memories that remain as vivid as if they'd happened yesterday, though it was twenty-some odd years ago.

It was the happiest times of my life.

Fate though, had other plans. You see, while I was working hard at doing all these gigs, and helping others out as best I could, a Gaffer I worked with introduced me to a friend of his. He said the person needed help with some electrical and remodeling. The person seemed genuinely in need, so I agreed.

The first ignored warning sign I should have heeded was the fact that at the time the Gaffer we worked with had a serious alcohol and cocaine issue — so much that we'd have to bail him out on shows he either nearly blew off, or passed out on—so whoever he recommended... well, you know.

The second was hearing a bit later these whispered rumors that this person had not only been his supplier, but that of a number of producers and performers up in the Hollywood Hills. Yet, that inner altruistic-ninny of mine dismissed such notions, right up to the point I found that person's body in their home. Instead of calling the police, I decided to check and see if my girlfriend and her family were okay, and then called my "friends" up to see what was going on, and what I should do. (Mind you, these are those who were later to be found to be the person's "clients.") Yep, yours truly was vying to become the Wally of the Century back then. As I waited for a return call from one of the blokes, it seemed they had another agenda or two. There was a knock at the door, which opened to a half-dozen police with guns drawn, screaming at me to "freeze" and "get down." Both seemed contradictory, don't you think? I knew right then that I was about to possibly become "the thing that couldn't leave."

My world as I knew it was about to be crushed.

So, here I was in County Jail. I awaited trial for four and a half years thinking that it would all blow over. Hell, I was miles away from the crime, and knew nothing of what had happened. Surely those who I had helped would be there for me, right?

You meet all sorts there, on both sides of the law. There were celebrities, dope fiends (sometimes combined!), gang members, drunks—you had it all. It seemed that the only ones you could depend on or truly trust were the cockroaches and mice that infested your dim surroundings. There would be screams all around you—men getting raped, others throwing excrement at anything that moved, or smearing themselves with it. Some would kill themselves or others often for something as small as a wrong glance or a candy bar.

Yet as I awaited trial, something still remained ...

You see, I make these Christmas trees ...

WHEN THE HOLIDAYS approached, I would take a *Readers Digest,* or some booklets or pamphlets that visiting zealots would leave behind, and fold them into the shape of a tree, more geometric than not (Picasso had nothing on these!). With some chewing gum or candy foil liberated from the trash, some toilet paper and string (from the underwear you were issued), and glue made from tooth-paste, there would emerge a little six- or eight-inch tree, resplendent with star and ornaments, hanging from the cell bars. That little guy seemed to cheer people up. Even the deputies and a visiting Arch-bishop seemed to take joy from the sight. Christmas night would come, and there I'd lay on my bunk, gazing up at it in the pale light seeping in from the tier outside—dreaming of that time long ago.

The attorney, the investigator all said it'd all be over soon: there was proof of my innocence, and they don't send the innocent to prison, right? All I had to do was just trust them.

Shortly after my conviction, I was shipped to a prison in the high desert where it was determined that I would spend the rest of my life. My girlfriend and her family? Gone. Back to New Zealand. All my good friends had cut me loose—some family as well. The publicity was just too much, and they had their own lives to live.

So here I was, trying to hash out some sort of appeal, and adjust to what might well be my permanent home. The time came around again when the holidays were nearing and thoughts again drifted more often than not back to home and hearth, and loved ones missed. I couldn't just give up. I just couldn't.

So, here I was contemplating another toothpaste and paper creation, when an idea came to me. After hours of trial and error, I'd found that one could cut, roll, and twist little pieces of paper to resemble tiny branches—the actual branches of a Scotch-Pine or Fir tree at that! Voila! Next came a base, a stem, some tape, aluminum foil, and after about six to seven hours of steady work there would spring this tiny little tree, which not only looked somewhat authentic, but became a local craze in the housing unit and the facility. People seemed to change physically and emotionally whenever they were given one of these—I couldn't be satisfied just doing one for myself. There were many others in the same fix, or even worse, as I was in. Especially when I gave these away as gifts, for free, and not as some prison "hustle," others and their families loved them. It took them back to memories of their own, I suppose.

When you totalled them all up, I must have made and given away close to four hundred or so of these little guys to inmates, free-persons, and mailed out to family members (even those who never even sent a card—it was Christmas, right?). All couldn't believe that such could come out of a place like this, for some reason— something I still don't get.

You know, I still get asked why I do this every year, and each time I say "Because it's Christmas." Yet, there is another reason that I have never shared with anyone—the only reason, in fact.

It's because of something I've always lived by and believed in no matter where I was, or what the situation I might be in: That despite all the heartache, the loss, and all the uncertainty that one finds in the challenges that one has to face, there is always that innate goodness, that little child in all of us laying beneath the branches gazing upward to something filled with light, with magic, and with hope.

You see, I make these Christmas trees...

OLE' HUM

I'VE HEARD that the sum total of one's existence is comprised of past memories, the current day physicality and future potential. Traumatic memory usually dictates how we view the world. Past woes often dominate the topics of most human interaction. I grew up in a violent and chaotic household. Although I have fond memories of some of my childhood, most of my days growing up were centered around surviving my father's psychosis. But, unknowingly, his behavior prepared me for prison. His disorganized philosophy helped make it an easy transition from the free world into the realms of the penal system.

I have been in prison now for twenty-seven years and most of my memories would be considered nightmares by an average person. My childhood and prison memories consist of horror and laughter. Seeing the family dog pummeled with a shovel, then decapitated. Visions of blood-soaked chambray prison shirts. Being whipped with a razor strap for spilling milk. Seeing a fifteen pound dumbbell being repeatedly hammered into the skull of a snitch. Seeing a black man hanging in a tree. Watching someone get tossed off of the fifth tier onto cement, flattening their face beyond recognition. Bone crusher knives buried in the chests of welchers. Watching helplessly as rogue cops drag someone away, never to be seen again. Coming home and seeing my cell mate hanging from the ceiling.

All of these things in my mind are topped by the relentless energy to be free opposed by the enormous weight of guilt for my crime: these are juxtaposed, intertwined forces of equal might. As a lifer, it takes years, if ever, for the sentence of never being free to burn into your core. Even if you're lucky enough to 'get over it,' you are reminded daily of your insignificant existence. The carnage and snuffing out of humanity dance around in your mind much like a war veteran suffers from post traumatic stress syndrome. Seeing dead and butchered bodies has a way of making one feel the rawness of life and how precious and fragile we all are.

In this sea of crimson memories, pre and post incarceration, there were special times of hope that have transformed and helped me maintain a sense of sanity: Warm rays of light in a cold, dark cataclysm of hopelessness and despair. The first fish that I caught in Alaska. The first touchdown I scored in the Pop Warner League. My first time with a woman. The birth of my children. Seeing a friend make parole. These are all great things that I have witnessed, but, for me, my greatest epiphany came in a quarter ounce package of feathered acrobatic energy. My saving grace, my special light, my buoy of sanity in a sea of madness comes from the memory I have of my best friend, Ole' Hum. My memories, before Ole' Hum came into my life, were filled with cold grays and sounds of discord. The only exception would be the birth of my kids. Ole' Hum taught me how to see—taught me how to hear and feel the sounds of the universe.

During the course of my social rejection, I have had the privilege of raising several types of animals. The animal world is very honest and forthright. So, in an ocean of human treachery and violence, animals have always been an oasis of wholesomeness. Ole' Hum was a bumble-bee hummingbird. He and his D.O.A. sibling were brought to me by a guard who found them in their tiny nest near the prison parking lot. I was known as the bird man of Folsom because of the dozen or so sparrows that I had raised over the years. Ole' Hum was so very tiny and weak that I was sure that he would meet the same fate as his nest mate. But, his will to live was larger and stronger than any creature I had ever seen.

As he grew, we became very attached and it was obvious that he was a very special friend. I was at the center of his universe and though I didn't know it at the time, Ole' Hum was my savior. His tiny feathers came in and grew fast and before I knew it, he was airborne. His instinctive maneuvering wasn't nearly as impressive as his attitude. He was very attentive and concerned with me being happy. In his own way, he would insist that I be happy like him. He knew when I was angry or down and wouldn't stop until I was with him. As he became an adult, his iridescent plumage flickered like a neon night light at a cheap motel and I can still hear the wind being cut around him as he motored his wings. His aerial acrobatics of fluttering movements dance in my mind and my heartbeat increases.

When people saw me smile during the day, most of the time Ole' Hum was the cause. His special attention forced me to look deep into myself. Surrounded by mayhem and death, a world of cold steel and deceit, a society of gangs and insanity—a place where suicide isn't thought of as crazy, just weak—I found my center. I felt the meaning of happiness for the first time in my life. I found the meaning of life and it was forced on my by my little feathered friend. Every day that I have been alive, society has tried to force me into a mold. Whether I fit in it or not, force was the only way. "We are higher than the animals," they would say. "We are better than the dirt and sky." "We are the only beings with souls and the only ones to have life after death." "We are privileged life forms." Yet, we are the ones polluting the air. We kill for the fun of killing. We let our greed control us.

Chief Seattle put it the best when he said, "How can you have your heads so far up in the clouds when your feet still touch the ground?" Ole' Hum was a sage teacher. He was more alive in one heartbeat than most men are their whole lives. His connection to life helped me realize that we are all connected. We are all a part of this earth and are bonded together like the pebbles of sand at the beach. Our blood flows in our veins and through the rivers. Our breath connects with all of the air in the atmosphere. Our hearts beat as one. The world that man has created :nakes a loud crashing sound, but the heartbeat of Ole' Hum beats louder still. His fluttering cry is deafening for those who wish to listen. He was the ambassador for earth.

I have since adapted his happy-go-lucky attitude and it helps me endure the thoughts of being in prison forever. Ole' Hum is my champion, my healer, my lighthouse of sanity. We all find our place in time, some on their death beds, some times in little small feathered packages. Tomorrow I will wake up to the clanking sounds of my ruin. I will walk to the chow hall and choke down the swill of the day. I will watch as the pill line grows with every new fish that hits the line. And I will smile. Around every corner, in the shadows, Ole' Hum chops away at the air around him teasing me with his freedom and wisdom. I will always smile and chase the freedom with happiness. Bent, but not broken, I follow the leader. Long live Ole' Hum. You will always be free and so will I.

JOHN PURUGGANAN

INCARCERATION WITHOUT REHABILITATION: TRUTH AND CONSEQUENCES

LIFE IS FILLED with consequences. It's no different here, in prison. But enter the gates of a state penitentiary, you're in a whole other world. There ought to be a sign: Check Your Humanity At The Door. Pick it up on your way out, if you ever get out of here—alive.

Of course there is no such sign. A belief that prisoners are actually human would be required. I get it. Really, I do. Before I came to prison I didn't know people who even knew people who'd been to prison. I never thought about prisoners. I do recall my basic sentiment: "To hell with 'em. They're lucky to be alive, thieving, raping, murdering bastards." All I knew was that they were in there for a reason. Do whatever you want to 'em, just keep 'em locked up, is how I felt. I worked two jobs, paid my taxes. My kids needed food, clothes. I had rent to think about, gas, electric, car insurance. Methodologies pertaining to the warehousing of criminals never entered my mind. I didn't care. Why should I?

Why should you?

I care now, naturally. I'm in prison.

A California State Prison.

If at all possible, one really should check his humanity in at the door—it will not serve you in this environment. Conscience has no place here: it will only plague you with guilt, if not cost you your life. Right-doing and wrong-doing are no longer questions of morals and values. All value is reduced to the least common denominator. Survival.

Each day you step out of your cell you must be physically and mentally prepared for sudden conflict, at alert, ready to fight. Anyone might be gunning for you. Everyone is a potential enemy. You're surrounded by bitter men who feel they have nothing to live for, nothing to lose. Men whose greatest fear is to be viewed as someone who is weak. Acts of violence are committed simply to gain a primal sense of respect.

The strongest survive.

Predator or prey.

This is the mentality.

This is the reality.

Guards are trained in effect that you are subhuman, that you hold no more value than an animal. They treat you like an animal—and why not? You certainly act like one. There is a direct correlation between the way one is treated and the way one acts. It makes no difference. You are an animal.

Pavlov's dog could provide some insight here. This type of conditioning, day in and day out, it does something to a man. Nonetheless, these are the wages of his sin, the consequence of his criminal action.

Perhaps rightly, justly so.

Still and all, what are the consequences when he paroles? Hopefully, after years of living like an animal, he is able to pick up his humanity on the way out the door. When he paroles into your community. Ideally, when Joe Convict steps outside these gates and feels the sunshine warm his face, the free breeze tousling his close-cropped hair, he will instantaneously transform into a positive-thinking individual, ready to reenter the free world equipped with the skills and the frame of mind he will need to be a contributing member of society. An upstanding citizen. No longer criminally inclined, a psychologically sound person with no potential disorders only fortified by years of living in an atmosphere of fear and violence.

With any luck he won't feel the need to self-medicate with a shot of heroin, a blast of crack, a line of coke, or a shot of speed to help him shake that prison hell he just left behind. Any luck he'll get a good nights' sleep, and not be up all night with visions of all those prison stabbings playing over and over in his head like a visual broken record. Well, not all the stabbings. Just the one. The one where his best buddy Jimmy lay in a pool of blood, looking directly at him with a confused look on his face. Stupid Jimmy. He wasn't going to make it on the inside anyway. He was slow in the head and stubborn like a child. When told that he had to stab that snitch or get stabbed himself—he just didn't get it.

Joe told himself he had no other choice but to kill Jimmy, just like George had to kill Lenny in Of Mice And Men. "It ain't right to let another man kill your own dog." So he did it. He walked right up to his best friend and slit his throat. He then glanced at the point men: a cock-sure convict sporting a long braid, another guy in state blues steam-pressed to the nines, and a muscle head bursting out of a grimy tank top; each man gave a slight nod in turn. Joe handed off the shank, took a seat at a pinochle game in progress. He looked over at Jimmy, lying on the dayroom floor, and watched as he bled out, looking right back at him, trying to figure out what the heck had just happened.

Joe still tries to convince himself that what he did to Jimmy was honorable, but deep down he knows the truth. He did what he did because he knew that if he didn't, he would be stabbed. It was a simple matter of self-preservation and had nothing to do with honor. All the stabbings after that meant nothing to him. He became inured to seeing guys getting their heads stomped in, to helping stomp guys heads, to getting his own head stomped in. But Jimmy, stinking retard, didn't belong in here. He did steal that car. He didn't plan on stealing it: "But it was just sittin' there runnin', nobody in it."

Joe was not implicated in Jimmy's death, though he did get caught, a number of times, serving other men varied degrees of grief with a shank. Those endless days and nights in the hole, pacing like a caged animal. He feared sleep. It was always bad sleep, prison nightmare. He didn't find the striking images themselves particularly disturbing: swirling scenarios of shanks ripping flesh; broken bones rupturing skin; fingers gouging out eyeballs; distorted, agonized faces. Not even the grossly excessive blood which splattered his vision like so many buckets of red hurled against a windshield was distinctly nightmarish. It was the way these images flash-scrolled and intermittently paused before his eyes, creating an intense sensation of drowning. And the screams. Ear-splitting screams of horror that he'd never heard in real life, only in his nightmares, and precisely when the flitting images sped forward. With a gasping gulp for air he'd awaken, wet, drenched in cold sweat, reinforcing the drowning terror. As he lay there, hyperventilating, drifting across that fogged landscape which exists between consciousness and sleep, for a moment, just a moment, he was glad to be here, in prison, and not in that suffocating whirlpool of whiplash images he'd just escaped.

Joe feels like he hasn't slept in years. But he'll rest easy tonight. He's out of prison. He'll get up in the morning and go out and find that job. He doesn't have enough money to get high anyway. Before he left the joint he had to pay for a pair of sweats to have something to wear. Then there was his bus fare, and when he finally rolled into town he bought a pair of Levis, a chambray shirt (it didn't occur to him that he'd just purchased a civilized version of state blues), a pair of Nike knock-offs, and a burger and a Coke. Out of his $200 gate money, he has just enough left to buy a six-pack of beer. That's what he needs: a few beers to clear his head. Then he can focus on amending his current financial predicament.

A quick convenient store robbery would be sweet—shame he doesn't have a gun. Those credit card scams he learned in the joint were slick, if only he had a computer. Mugging someone is hardly worth the trouble. Most people don't carry much cash, and a person can wear only so much jewelry.

He isn't worried though, no more than a wild predator worries about its day. Just a few more beers. It'll come to him. Mmm, now that was refreshing, hit the spot. Got a good buzz going now. Ah, and here it is, his economic uncertainty suddenly made certain. Get a baseball bat, or a big piece of wood. No, no, a metal pipe. Lead. Yeah ... feels good in his hand, not too big, not too small, just right, a good grip. Man is he hungry. He smiles to himself—two birds with one stone, so to speak. Guess who's coming to dinner? Commemorate a little old fashioned home invasion. It'll go over smooth. He never got a chance to take any anger management classes in prison, but he can control all that pent-up rage.

A disturbing illustration.

A horrifying reality.

Society. Taxpayers. YOU. Deserve better than this.

Criminal activity wounds society as a whole. Healing begins with justice. Persons convicted of criminal conduct are incarcerated, the consequence of misdemeanor and felonious action. What most people do not realize is that what goes on behind prison walls directly affects them. Once a criminal is behind bars, the average citizen is satisfied that justice has been served. He does not realize the injustice of incarceration without rehabilitation — the injustice being committed against himself and the public at large.

The "just lock 'em up" mentality is exactly what those who are in the business of incarceration thrive on. While rehabilitation is undeniably good for society, it has the opposite affect for the business of incarceration. Rehabilitation goes against the prime objective: Expansion. Build more prisons and maintain—at the very least—100% occupancy. No different than hotels overbooking to insure maximum occupancy, it is imperative for prisons to keep the beds filled. Business is as business does. Business does what is necessary to succeed.

On the other hand, the general public has a right to challenge the practices a business employs when it infringes upon their well-being, their very safety; especially when they are the ones footing the bill. For decades—centuries—prison policies have been exclusively negative and punitive, policies which are a proven detriment. Historically prisoners are released even more dangerous than when they entered prison.

The solution: The Honor Program.

Tried, tested, and proven effective. The following is an excerpt from a briefing which was prepared by Senator Gloria Romero, who chairs the California Senate Public Safety Committee:

The Honor Program, created in 2000 by prisoners and non-custody staff with the desire to lower violence, crime, racism, and drug use, has proven to be very effective. It is located on the Facility-A (which houses about 600 men) at the Level IV maximum security California State Prison, Los Angeles County (CSP-LAC).

—Prisoners must appy to participate in the program. They are screened, must have a clean record, and must state a desire to commit to more demanding criteria, including abstaining from violence, racism, gang involvement, and drug use. (Random drug testing is part of the program.)

—The Honor Program requires each prisoner to create an "Individual Development Plan" to achieve self-improvement goals. Prisoners agree to take responsibility for their own personal growth and transformation, and are involved in programs or activities that address emotional, psychological, social and/or vocational health.

—The Honor Program allows prisoners to have a choice between the negative group punishment model or personal responsibility and individual accountability. It clearly separates those who really want to change and improve.

—The Honor Program has demonstrated the desire of prisoners to help others, to give back to the community, and make amends for past wrongdoings. Tens of thousands of dollars has been raised for, and thousands of contributions have been made by, Honor Program prisoners to non-profit organizations, Toys for Tots and similar groups, the poor around the world by eyeglass refurbishing programs, and many other areas of help for the needy.

—In its first year of operation The Honor Program at CSP-LAC:
    -Saved the taxpayers of California $200,000
    -Reduced weapons offenses by 88% and violence by 85%

—In its six years of operation, the Honor Program has functioned without a single major violent incident, with savings of millions of dollars to the state of California.

—With greater official support, so much more is possible through the Honor Program. Many positive opportunities have been dashed as a result of lack of desire to explore safe, workable, and economically sensible options.

LIFE IS FILLED with consequences. Incarcerate a man in an environment of hate, violence, racism, cruelty, dishonor, disrespect, despair, over time he will embody all the above.

By the same token, place him in an atmosphere of hope, encouragement, responsibility, accountability, respect, tolerance, honor, trust, peace, and it will rub off on him.

But what about punishment? These men have been convicted of crimes against society, against people, against you. Shouldn't they be punished? It's not supposed to be a walk in the park. Where is the punishment?

Incarceration *is* punishment. When a man is incarcerated he is stripped of all freedom. He is put in a cell—a 2-man cell, a 50-man cell. His cell is a cage; he has no privacy. His cage is locked; he leaves his cage only when permitted; he takes a shower only when permitted. He is strip-searched/skin-searched/cavity-searched, his entire body examined for hidden contraband and evidence of violence—swollen knuckles, scratches, contusions— concluding with the ultimate indignity: he is ordered to cough while the beam of a flashlight are aimed between the spread cheeks of his buttocks. These represent just few of the physical punishments which define incarceration.

I know a prisoner who received a picture last week— a picture his stepfather found on the internet. The picture was of his baby boy. This was the first time he'd seen him (or any of his six children) in 19 years. The last time he saw him was in the county jail, his tiny hand touching the glass which separated him from his father's hand on the other side. He doesn't know if his son ever received a single letter he wrote, doesn't know if he is aware that the last letter he sent, over a decade ago, was returned with no forwarding address. He doesn't know if his baby boy, who is now this handsome young stranger staring back at him from a university basketball roster, knows that he has a father who loves him, who never stopped loving him, and is sorry beyond words for not being there for him, for not being the father he deserved.

Incarceration.

Allow me to offer qualified assurance. Every prisoner will receive layers of punishment, regardless of policy or program. Truly.

The real question: Is California—is America—ready to demand justice for themselves by demanding that genuine rehabilitation be readily obtainable in all of their prisons? Given a choice, the majority of prisoners would sign on for a chance to improve themselves. What needs to be realized is that rehabilitation cannot occur in a violent atmosphere. Trying to teach someone how to live a more productive and rational life in the midst of daily violence and chaos is impossible. This is why rehabilitation has ultimately failed in the past, to the lamentable degree it has been attempted.

I have been incarcerated since 1989. To my shame and remorse, I killed a man. The consequence of my actions has me serving a life sentence without the possibility of parole. For the past five years I have been an active participant in the Honor Program. In all the years of my experience on traditional prison yards, whenever someone was paroling I never heard anyone say they would not return. Such a claim would have been laughable. Everyone came back—it was just a question of when.

Here, on the Honor Yard, men approach parole with a completely different attitude and frame of mind. Different because they live in a positive environment, in the confines of a program which encourages channeling personal (and collective) energies to achieve worthwhile goals. They have committed themselves to respect, to excellence, to personal growth.

The men here come from all walks of life. Many of them come from inner-city neighborhoods and impoverished backgrounds. Decent educations and exposure to the arts was not a common occurence. The Honor Program offers a wide range of arts, education, self-help, and vocational courses. Minds are opened to new ideas, new possibilities. With previously unexplored left-brain territories stimulated, men here have discovered talents they never knew they possessed. Many are now enrolled in college, taking courses through correspondence. As self-esteem and confidence blossom, grown men are inspired to change. They want to change. More importantly they come to believe they can change. They want to live better lives than what eventually, inevitably led them to prison.

The Honor Program at Facility A, California State Prison Los Angeles County is a proven model for rehabilitation. It should be duplicated throughout the state and across the nation. The cost to operate this type of prison program? Less than a typical prison yard. The benefits of parolees being released from a positive environment? Priceless.

COLE M. BIENEK

HOMESICK

Hello there. Can you hear me?
What do I look like, how do I smell?
Is there something you'd like to say to me,
or would you just like to stare?
Maybe throw me a handful of cheese-
flavoured popcorn and watch as I carefully
collect each precious scrap, stowing some
in my blue pocket for late night snacking.

Surely you can see the moat between us.
I can't. It's only on your side. A narrow defile
hastily constructed of irrational fears,
braced with the salted iron spokes of
communal amnesia.
Did you forget that I am you and you are me?
Manicured lawns, two cars and suburban soccer leagues
or chain links and walls around crumbling urban schools
pockmarked with divots where gun blasts seared the air.
I remember when you closed your eyes and looked away from me,
then glanced back to purposefully see through me.
Fortunato couldn't have built a stronger wall among us,
no better cask of ancient wine used for bait.

I stepped from the sidewalk, away from you and nearly died
        under a bus
while you stayed within the linear pedestrian flow.
The other side of the street is still the same for you and I—
I just had to negotiate more traffic to get there.

Now I sit here all day, banging on an invisible,
but breakable plastic window—can you hear me?
What would you do if you could?
When this bubble breaks can I come home?

COLE M. BIENEK

AD-OPTED

I was three days old,
a tiny thing wrapped in sterile hospital swaddle
offered to the fates by a mother
too occupied by other cares and worries
to make room for baby.
Three days old, taken from my little plastic crib,
chosen by a mother with room in her heart for baby.

Three years old, running away from father,
a drunk? Perhaps he beat her.
He was alone with me for a day and a half
until mother escapes with baby.

I don't think I've been as happy since.
A day and a half—a drunk miscreant
alone with baby. I wonder,
did I laugh or cry?

COLE M. BIENEK

AN ARROW FLIES

Would that I were as an arrow in flight,
Supremely directed and energetic.
I'd not make detours, or become lost on the way;
My tasks, I'd accomplish without delay.

But— what peace is that, to be sped
onward toward unseen destinies;
without choice. Without chance to fail.
No, to be an arrow is only half of life,
unconscious primacy of result.

C O L E M . B I E N E K

SOMETIMES THE STARS

Step back from the brink
draw breath and think
blink away the mists
grind your eyes with fists—
full of sand
is it possible to understand,
with Zen archery precision
the heart's decision made
seven lifetimes before Adam
      believed—
      Was it always Eve?
Left behind to stir the pot
making darn sure that the stew was hot.

I slipped and slid; a confused Adam indeed
squinted in the sun, caught the
hand of my Eve.

Preview the stars and late night
trips to the outskirts of Mars
where she deigns to flirt,
twirl her skirt; outshine the day;
tiptoe along the Milky Way.

We rode Halley's Comet thrice round home;
swam in the pools of Jupiter—
through the deserts of Io we trod—
laughed and played when we understood the

face of God.

Extraordinarily blessed, seven times seven
grades above—
for love—and Love brought
experience what Love hath wrought
like puppies across dewy grass
for the first time
wet noses and innocence
hearts without pretense
only presence
and presents.

COLE M. BIENEK

DISTANT SHOWER

Warm summer wind catches
hold of fragrant cactus blossoms,
carries delicate scents miles
across the sands.

The rains arrived overnight;
and the rising sun
awoke a billion colors from
protective slumber.

Clear to the distant, hazy horizon
the Desert shouts and dances—
utter joy rouses sleepy critters
from their cool, shaded burrows.

There, in a blue-tinted hollow
lay two forms—
one against the other;
soft curves complementing
rigid angles.

They doze upon an ancient, color-faded blanket;
hand in hand
lips to ear
whispering gentle wind-caressed
promises;
ever remembered across fountain'd valleys.

C O L E   M .   B I E N E K

THERE IS A SEASON:
A PERFECT STORM IN CALIFORNIA'S
PRISON SYSTEM

TRAVIS WALKED across the crowded prison yard, lead-heavy ice weighing his steps. Five hundred sets of eyes monitored his steady progress toward the housing unit. At nineteen years old, Travis was a little boy all over again. Nobody spoke to him -- it was not yet time for talk. This was judgement time; time for determinations and pre-suppositions. Time to label him based upon appearance. Young, white, shaved head—obviously a skinhead. Behind the cover of the gray stone walls, appearances will convict and re-sentence a man with a full measure of mindless brutality. Travis met their stares until debilitating fear devoured what little sense of self remained. Passing a knot of Crips working out on pull-up bars and sit-up benches, he kept his eyes facing straight ahead, avoiding any eye contact. County jail experience taught him a harsh lesson about how a chance meeting of eyes could lead to a flurry of fists and boots.

Just before entering the dreary stone cellblock, four whites crossed his path. " 'Sup youngster," said a bald, heavily tattooed man, with no hint of welcome.

"Hey," Travis answered as he walked through the bulky steel doorway. The heaviness of two-hundred caged souls oppressive—he felt as if he were walking along the ocean floor with a million tons of water pressing down, stealing his breath.

I remember my own first walk onto a prison yard twenty-one years ago; the same look of sheer, tightly concealed terror pinched my face. I failed, just as Travis had, to conceal my fear beneath a mask of courage and toughness. I shook like a dog in the pound for two hours in the dubious safety of my cell. Now, all these years later I was one of the regs, a veteran of several riots, survived years on lockdown, thirty-seven months in the hole, and a couple attempted stabbings. Now I live a life of relative safety on the Honor Program— a single facility representing a refuge from the daily madness which characterizes the Califomia prison system, bursting at the seams and endemically dysfunctional.

I turned away from the window and back to work, typing reports for a baby-faced Correctional Lieutenant half my age. Through the window above my desk I watch prisoners come and go. I see old-timers resigned to their fate; regulars gearing up for a fight; and first-termers staring at the ground, shock silent. I watched the same guy, Sam, come and go three times in the last year. But Travis—his face stuck with me.

I was Travis once. Nineteen years old and thrust into the bladed maelstrom of hatred, drugs and violence. I fed at the trough, ran with the wolves, regressed to a more primal thing, concerned only with surviva.l I'd lain awake in my bunk all through the night, fearing that when the cell door opened in the morning I'd meet the imper-sonal end of a rusted homemade knife.

Being young and thin and emotionaly thirteen, I quickly learned not to swim against the prevailing current, ever-mindful that the cur-rents would change, often in midswim. Someone who was 'A' List in the morning could make a slight error in judgement and find him-self full of holes, stuffed unceremoniously beneath the stairs.

There are rules and rules; the administration has theirs, and the prisoners have their own. Break the guards rules and I'd lose what little privileges I had. Violate the wrong prisoners rule and I'd be quickly and viciously punished. As a youngster I received a certain amount of leeway, but the leaming curve was sharp. There was no making the same mistake twice.

I turned twenty on the maximum security yard in Pelican Bay state prison. At the time it was the highest security facility in the state. Known as the White House or simply, "The Bay," transfer there went a long way in establishing your reputation as one of the worst of the worst. For a birthday celebration I drank a half-gallon of homemade wine and had a nice shot of heroin.

Our yard was on lockdown because a man had been found on the weight pile with his face bashed in. Eight cameras, fifty guards, ten rifle-toting gunners and five-hundred prisoners all made the same statement: "I saw nothing."

The victim, New York Red, had made the unfortunate mistake of raising his hand—volunteering—to stab another prisoner, then changed his mind at the last second.

Big no-no. One didn't volunteer, one was volunteered.

Red was on the decline bench, a weight-lifting exercise where the lifter lays upside down on an angled bench and presses the weight upwards. In the middle of his set someone walked over and dropped an eighty-pound pig iron dumbbell on his head. To make matters worse, they even tied Red's bootlaces to the pole beneath the bench.

The guards initially noticed something amiss when the normally packed weight pile was suddenly empty. All prisoners were ordered to lie facedown in the mud as the guards walked over to see what was the matter. They didn't actually react with any kind of urgency until they saw all the blood. In a scene worthy of the best Stooges flick, they picked him up and tried to run to the clinic, but his laces were tied to the bench and they nearly dropped him. For refusing to stab another man, Red is permanently brain damaged—walks with a slight limp and can't pronounce the letter "T."

I drank until it all went away. And when that failed to work anymore I conjured an opiate induced stupor.

Six months later, my hand was raised. But not to stab—only to "regulate" someone—to beat him badly. The guy, Richard, disrespected his black neighbors by playing his radio too loud. Mindful of Red's punishment, I didn't even think of backing out of my "volunteering."

I followed Richard to his cell. The building was hushed; its occupants silent, sitting on the edge of their metaphorical seats. My hands shook, my breathing shallow. Richard was easily a hundred pounds and four inches my senior. As we passed beneath the stairs, I dropped a left hook on his jaw—a one-in-a-thousand shot. He dropped like the Russian economy. Better yet, several other prisoners watched me do it. My legend was born, such as it was. I kicked him a few times with little effect and strolled away, high as a kite. My revelry lasted far into the night, augmented by cocaine and heroin.

"Good job, youngster," Nazi Bob, the yard boss "shotcaller" congratulated me. I accepted the handshake a little nervously, Nazi Bob was a hulk of a man, a leftover from teutonic prehistory. Six-four and three hundred twenty pounds, and a member of the five-hundred club—meaning he could bench press five hundred pounds.

Three weeks later the war was on. Blacks and whites. Let the doors be the bell. A radio played too loud after nine p.m. was once again the culprit. Two whites, Cowboy and Arkansas, were up late drinkin'and blastin' the Hank Williams Jr. Their neighbors, a pair of lifer East Coast Crips, asked them politely to turn down the music, to"which Arkansas reponded, "Shut up nigger."

In the morning, C-Nutt and Bolo stabbed Cowboy and Arkansas so many times the crime report listed the wounds as, "Too numerous to count."

Ten minutes after the initial incident, five blacks were stabbed in the dining hall; followed by two whites; followed by three more blacks. The first day, seven men went to the hospital.

We were locked down for six months. Every day, me and my cellie rose at 5:30 a.m., checked our knives, put on our boots and prepared to die. We took on airs, pretended to be the genetic inheritors of the barbaric bloodlust of the Celts and Vikings.

The cell doors, operated remotely by a guard in the control booth, would often open at unpredictable times; an unfortunate "malfunction" which always resulted in a cell of whites and a cell of blacks being opened. Blood ran freely, and fear stained the block like a rotten thing, rancid and hot. The long days were punctuated by cadence calls of the prisoners doing unified calisthenics in their cells. One had to maintain their physical conditioning—you never knew when your ticket would get punched. Daily, the block grew eerily quiet around noon; everyone was glued to the TV watching soap operas. Sometimes TV land could transport us away from our concrete boxes for 23 1/2 hours a day.

I slept little that six months and aged visibly. Late at night, lying on my bunk, I stared at the ceiling and wondered when it would end.

Two weeks before the lockdown ended, my cellie and I were caught with homemade knives and sentenced to time in the Security Housing Unit (S.H.U. pronounced 'Shoe'). The SHU was California's Supermax. A super high-tech construction of concrete and steel designed to strip away any last vestiges of humanity and resistance prisoners may possess. Devoid of any human contact other than one's cellmate, the psychological torment bored deeply into the core of the psyche. Symptoms of Post-Traumatic Sress Disorder (PTSD) set in: insomnia, suicidal ideation, delusions, and eating disorders were as common as the oversized June bugs crawling beneath our cell doors.

Any time I left the "pod," as the cell blocks were named, I was shackled, hand and foot. Without the ability to read and draw, I would likely have succumbed to one of the myriad madnesses rampaging through the darkened, echoing corridors. So disorienting were these halls that I lost all sense of direction. For all I knew we could've been two miles underground. We told time by the TV news or by which meal was brusquely thrust through the food port.

I lived months upon months in daily terror of the guards known statewide for their propensity to randomly open the cells of opposing ethnicities and gangs; to the notorious and deadly prison gang members who viewed me and my cellie as nothing more than cannon fodder—expendable and amusing, nothing more. The gangs were able to direct the opening of certain cells, so if I found myself in the unfortunate position of offending or inadvertently disrespecting one of them, I could find myself alone on the tier facing two men with knives.

I didn't realize it then, but drug abuse drove everything I did. If it could be injected, drank, smoked, snorted or sniffed—I used it. Ten years later, I lay on a cold steel bunk in an icy cell in the hole of a prison in the desolate northern high desert of Califomia. I amounted to nothing; my life represented nothing. Lucky, I was, even to be alive. Owing only to dumb luck or divine intervention—or both—the foot-long chunk of steel intended for my heart failed to penetrate my sternum. All I received was an angry bruise and the privilege of being single-celled in the hole.

My reckless past had caught up with me in the form of a collector sent to extract pain in lieu of unpaid dope debts. For years I'd been pretending to be a thug—stiffing dope dealers and daring them to do something about it. Eventually someone bought the wolf tickets I'd been selling. I left the hole after seven months with a slightly different attitude. Perhaps there was a different way.

My boss walked in, disturbing my daydreams. "You can go for the day, I know you wanna play in the softball tournament."

"Sure?" I asked, "I could stay and finish."

"Nah, go ahead." He checked if anyone else was in earshot. "I'm takin'the rest of the day off anyway." He coughed into his hand, twice, weakly. "I'm very sick."

"Okay then, see you on Monday." I was out and dressed for softball in minutes. Later that night, as the glow of winning wore off, I lay sleepless in my bunk, wondering how Travis' first night in prison was going; wondering what his four-thousandth night would be like — or if he'd even make it that far.

After my last stint in the hole, I tried to clean myself up. Tried on a religion or two. Got clean for a while. Fancied myself a changed man.

I fell off the wagon.

THE PROGRAMS in which I involved myself were only available when the facility remained off lockdown. Unfortunately, this wasn't often the case. In 1998, my facility was locked down for ten months. What little progress I made was lost. The lesson: rehabilitation is not possible in a war zone.

But, I'd had a taste of something special, of what could be. I just wasn't quite ready yet. In February, 2000, 1 was employed in one of the most desirable jobs in the prison system—an industries leadman and clerk. I made a little over a hundred dollars a month—a veritable fortune in an economy where I didn't have to pay room and board, or utilities. I was able to go to work when all the other prisoners were locked down.

On the day I discovered that the prison was slated to activate an "Honor Program," I received a raise. It was to be a yard where prisoners were required to be drug-free, give up gang affiliations, and meet increased behavioral expectations. In return, additional program opportunities would be provided.

In my mind's eye I envisioned a veritable utopia in prison, as far as comparisons go. Imagine a yard where prisoners choose to embrace change on the most personal levels possible; a yard where self-motivated prisoners and staff work together in order to reach a common goal. This was a thing I needed with all the panicky flailing of the drowning man seeking air.

I left my job, my comfortable life, and my friends, destined for the unknown. I had the dreams, and the desire—all I needed was the opportunity. Men who had known me for years said I was crazy, that to give up my cushy little job for a fantasy was just plain stupid. As it turns out, the Honor Program saved my life. Actually, to be more clear, it gave me a purpose. In a realm of violence, gang superiority, drug abuse, repression, chaotic rage—and hopelessness—the Honor Program is an oasis of hope for six hundred men. A foundation of sensible reality was built upon personal responsibility and growth. Men voluntarily took part in programs which the State had been trying to force them to do for years. Suddenly, rehabilitation became more than just a noun: it was put into action.

Career gang members and previously unreachable drug addicts changed their lives and became mentors. Prisoners were granted the opportunity to be responsible for themselves, their actions and their futures.

Prisoners became men.

California has the single most overtly racist prison system in the nation - if not the world. But, on the Honor Program, that bastion of senseless delineation was the first to fall. Men formed groups and friendships without the madness of racism on the point of a knife. Several interracial cell partnerships cropped up—an occurrence which on another yard would result in one or both of the men being stabbed, possibly killed.

Other barriers crumbled as well. The prisoners inbred animosity for staff virtually vanished. And, quiet as they would like to keep it, the staff members' antipathy for the prisoner class began to vanish as well. The onus was placed on the individual as opposed to the group.

Personally, my artistic talent flourished, and I learned how to teach. I know firsthand the transformational nature of the arts. Men will take risks with a painting or a piece of poetry that they otherwise wouldn't. I also discovered an affinity for writing—fiction mainly, of the swords 'n' sorcery, fantastical variety.

Mostly it is about being a part of the wave which will transform the prison system. I'm on the ground floor, front lines, with prisoners and staff who struggle for change in a system which predominantly opposes change. The prevailing correctional philosophy is a hundred years old—it's broken, and no amount of fervent wishing will fix it. Hope hangs on the actions of the few, as it often does throughout human history. In this case, it is the shoulders of the prisoners and staff of the Honor program which bear the burden.

For those who believe that their lives are not affected by the internal management of the correctional system, consider this: prisoners are going to return to society—some will be your neighbors. Do you want them paroling from gang-led, drug infested, cauldrons of hatred and violence?

Or do you want us to go through a voluntary program of self-investigation, drug counseling, victim awareness and anger management before being released?

At work on Monday, after bragging about softball exploits, I typed a transfer order moving Travis into my cell. Perhaps his time in prison could be spent in a productive, healing manner.

C O L E   M .   B I E N E K

IT CAME IN A BOTTLE

IT WAS LATE May and the call of summer was heard in the crack of baseball bats in schoolyards and sandlots, and in the croaking of frogs in hollows and creeks. Across America thirteen year old boys, and the occasional girl, responded to a trigger deeply embedded in their genetic makeup— like plants, they reacted to the lengthening days and increasing warmth. They skipped school and sought adventure along the byways and backwoods around the country. I was not immune to the call—no different was I than my fellows. Like lemmings, we snuck down silent hallways, past sleepy sentries and hall monitors. Our hearts beat so loud that they echoed off the stoic hallways as we pushed open double doors and stepped into afternoon sunshine.

Across playground fields we ran, through thick verdant grasses where grasshoppers fled in terror from our approach. Barely restrained joy threatened to burst from our lungs. Finally, we attained escape velocity. The border was breached.

Freedom! Our madness overflowed and we engaged in an impromptu dirt clod fight. No teams were chosen, no one was picked last, nobody wins or loses. The battle moved down creek side into a shallow, shaded depression speckled by errant sundrops and smelling of rich earth. Massive and ancient trees surrounded the banks and guarded our backs against the truant officer's keen eyes and the treachery of rival factions. Even our calls and shouts were muffled, absorbed into the wooden flesh of our austere allies.

"Darren! Hey, Dar-ren! Watch out!"

I ducked, because one should never look up when someone says watch out or heads up—all that will land you is a black eye or missing teeth. I tucked my chin and dove to the right, a huge chunk of something landed right behind me. It didn't explode like a proper clod though, only a thin scattering of dirt shooks free as it glanced off an exposed root.

"No rock-clods!" I shouted, enacting the rule. You see, everything was legal until someone made a rule, and all rules were reset the following day.

"No rocks! No rocks!" My rule echoed along the skirmish line and a new barrage of rock-free clods was loosed.

"Aarrgh!" The person who warned me paid dearly for his alarm. Wet sticky mud splattered onto my shorts and shoes.

"No mudpies!" the victim announced.

"No pies! No pies!" down the lines.

The battle raged, spies were caught and tortured, defectors taunted and lookouts revealed. Nobody knew who was winning, and nobody cared. Everyone fought for the same reason, although nobody but me could discern our true purpose: we fought because we had no choice. We fought because we were young and bulletproof. We fought because we could. And, we fought not with dirt clods— to us they were shiny, flaming ICBMs. The fate of the known world hung in the balance, and if not for us, civilization would be doomed to an endless slavery at the hands of commies or terrorists ... or better yet, aliens!

After a particularly vicious assault from the right, Tricia (the lone girl in our troupe) called a cease-fire. Now, there were only a very few legitimate reasons to call a cease-fire in the middle of a proper dirt-clod fight and this was a rule which was not reset the following day—it was a permanent, all-the-time rule. So, when Tricia shouted, we all stopped and looked around for the reason.

A few seconds later, Daniel, the one who warned me of the incoming rock-clod, walked over to Tricia and said, "Hey, what gives, huh? Where's the body?"

Daniel had been wanting to find a dead body for as long as we could remember, and the presence of a body was sufficient to declare a cease-fire.

"There's no body, stupid," said Rick. "We ain't gonna find no body out here, so give it up already."

Rick was our bully. Every group had one, and Rick was one of the best.

"Who're you callin' stupid, huh? People find bodies all the time."

"Yeah, on TV. You live on TV? Think this is CSI or somethin'?" Rick taunted.

"Shut up," Daniel fired back. He took a step towards Rick.

"What're you gonna do fatty? You gonna sit on me?" Rick laughs and tries to get the rest of us to join him. We don't.

"Knock it off, Rick," Matt said, walking toward Tricia. "Tricia's found something."

Matt was not necessarily our leader, but he did seem to come up with most of our ideas, and was the only one that Rick would listen to.

"What is it then," Rick asked, giving up on Daniel for the moment.

We all walked over to where Tricia stood halfway up the embankment on the other side of the creek. She was looking down at something partway buried in the dirt, an odd expression on her tanned face.

Matt got there first and knelt down by Tricia's feet, looking at the ground. I arrived next, followed by Rick and Daniel. Daniel was obviously still cross with Rick and made faces behind his back.

"I can see that, fatty," Rick said without looking back.

I almost laughed at the look on Daniel's face, but caught myself, lest I add to Daniel's misery.

"It's just a crappy bottle," Rick pointed out. Besides being our Bully, Rick was also our expert on cuss words, crap being his favorite. He said that as far as cuss words went, crap was as good as it gets; it could be used as a noun, verb or adjective, easily tailored for any cussing needs one may have.

"It's not just a bottle," Tricia pointed out, "at least not like any bottle I've seen before."

I leaned in for a better look, and it wasn't like any bottle I'd seen before either. The part I could see was an opaque greenish-yellow—mostly, but the colors shifted like those pictures that change when you move them around. The glass looked more solid than glass should be, as funny as that sounds, and it wasn't dirty at all—well, except for the part underground, of course. And there was a cork stuffed down in the mouth, like one of those message in a bottle, throw it in the ocean jobbies.

Matt reached out his hand to pick it up, and I instinctively scooted away. "I don't think that's such a good idea," I said.

"It's just a bottle, what's the big deal?" Matt replied.

A bottle it was, but definitely not just. As Matt's hand moved closer and closer, the shadows in the hollow grew a little deeper and to me it seemed the temperature dropped a bit.

"Yeah, I think Darren's right, you should leave it alone," Tricia said.

"You gotta be kiddin' me," Rick muttered. "Outta my way." He shouldered his way past me and before anyone could stop him, bent over and pulled the bottle from the ground. Tricia jumped out of the way of whatever was going to leap from the bottle and eat Rick.

The rest of us were frozen, unsure what price Rick was going to pay for his impatience.

A few seconds passed and when he was still standing there, Matt asked, "What does it feel like?"

"What does it feel like? A bottle, whatdya think it feels like, cottage cheese?" Rick laughed.

We all joined in for a laugh, the built-up tension dispersed by our cleansing laughter. Something nagged at me, though. The bottle dangled from Rick's hand, momentarily forgotten, except for me. I couldn't take my eyes off it. Its greenish opacity was hypnotic and drew my attention ever inward. As Rick laughed his arm swung back and forth and I tracked the path of the bottle. His thumb worried at the cork and it inched its way toward freedom. I tried to say something, to tell Rick not to do that, but my body refused orders from my brain. The sounds of laughter faded from my awareness and silence laid its cottony embrace across my shoulders. The cork fell and disappeared into the moist leaf litter. My breathing and heartbeat became the extent of my world. All else departed, forgotten completely. My vision swam, up became down and gravity flip-flopped. I wasn't aware that I'd fallen— could care less. My eyes were filled with the fantastic sight of a pair of tiny, topless faeries.

Being thirteen I had seen naked women in magazines. But none of that compared to the sight of the anatomically correct eight inch tall faeries. I squeezed my eyes shut, hard, until I saw little blooms behind my eyelids. I opened them expecting the hallucinations to be gone. Much to my surprise there were more of them, of both genders. At least a dozen now flitted and hovered about the branches above. I was mesmerized, caught in a spell so pure that I could do nothing but stare.

Each was so different and so perfectly formed, all different colors and shades. One hid behind a leaf and peeped her tiny head around the side. "It can see us," she said. Her voice was like the crystal tinkling of tiny bells.

"No, they can't see us," said another — a boyish voice.

"That one can." More tinkling bells from somewhere off to the right.

"No it can't. Watch, I'll show you."

The little faerie flew down until he was only a couple feet from the tip of my nose. He leaned with his tiny hand on his chin and with pursed lips announced, "See, nothing. You know how they react if they see us."

"I can see you," I ventured.

Perhaps I shouldn't have spoken, or maybe I should have just ignored them. Whatever it was, the faeries erupted into a frenzy of shouting and hectic flying. Like a colony of confused bees they flitted from leaf to leaf, hiding spot to hiding spot. Little tussles broke out over the right to prime locations.

Then they were gone.

I don't remember being asleep, but I recall waking up to Tricia's gentle prodding. "Darren ... Darren ... c'mon, wake up," she was saying. I kept my eyes closed and laid there in the rich dirt of the hollow. I was mesmerized by the water trickling around rocks in the creek to my left, and birds calling out to one another from treetop to treetop.

"He ain't sleepin'," Rick said.

I felt a shoe dig into my side, hard. 1 tried to ignore it but Rick managed to find a spot between ribs that made me twitch and laugh. How could something hurt as well as tickle?

"See," Rick said.

"Knock it off," Matt said.

I opened my eyes in time to see Matt pushing Rick away from me. Rick joined Daniel a few feet away, muttering something under his breath. Matt knelt down at my side next to Tricia. "Are you okay?" he asked.

I nodded and sat up, grimacing. For some reason I felt that it should hurt to sit up. "Yeah, I think so. What happened?"

Matt looked at Tricia and something passed between them. "What," I said.

"Nothin' happened. That's what," Rick said.

Matt stood and looked Rick down. Tricia turned her attention back to me. Quietly, she said, "Did you see anything?"

Faeries? Are you asking if I saw a band of little green, blue and orange faeries? Well, then ... yes, I did. Go ahead and toss me in the looney bin. Put me in that suit with backwards arms and strap me to a table. "Uh ... see anything?"

"Yeah," she said, "anything ... weird?"

"Weird?"

"Stop answering with a question, what did you see?" Tricia insisted.

She wasn't angry, Tricia was never angry with me, sometimes with Rick or Daniel — even Matt made her mad sometimes, but never me. I looked at my muddy knees and absentmindedly scratched at the right one. "Faeries," I said too softly to be heard.

"Hmm?" Tricia prompted, "I couldn't hear you."

"Faeries, I saw a buncha faeries okay!"

Rick started laughing. "Baby saw faeries! Baby saw faeries!"

"Shut up, Rick, you saw 'em too," Matt said.

" I didn't see nothin', 'specially no faeries."

"You're lyin', we all saw 'em," said Tricia.

"Yeah," Daniel echoed.

I stood up and joined my allies in defiance of Rick. It took only a few seconds for him to give in. "Alright, I saw 'em too."

"Maybe it was all just a hallucination. My brother sees stuff all the time that isn't there," Daniel offered.

"Yeah, that's 'cause he's high," Rick said. "What's our excuse?"

"Yeah, we're not high. Maybe it was just the light through the trees?" Matt suggested.

I thought that was a pretty stupid idea, especially coming from Matt, who usually had our best ideas. I didn't point that out though, because if you don't have something productive to offer you should keep your mouth shut. At least that was what grandpop said. Suddenly I wondered what happened to the bottle. I looked around and saw it, uncorked, lying in the leaf litter beneath a spreading oak. To me it looked like the bottle was radiating its own warm glow, kinda yellowish, and it beat with a faint pulse. I took a step toward it. It was the bottle, I knew, that had started everything. Where was the cork?

"What is it, Darren?" Matt asked.

"Huh?" I said, turning. "Oh, nothing." I looked at my knees again.

"C'mon, what is it?" Tricia said.

"Yeah, what's goin' on?" Daniel echoed.

"We all saw something, right?"

Tricia and Matt nodded, while Daniel and Rick remained somewhat passive.

"The cork ... when Rick flicked the cork out with his thumb, that's when it started."

"What started?" Daniel asked.

I stood up and brushed the leaves and debris from my clothes. Everyone was looking at me all of a sudden. I don't do well under pressure, I tend to stutter and allow myself to fade into the background. "I don't know," was all I could say.

"Here it is," Tricia said. I didn't know she'd wandered away.

"Maybe we should put it back in, huh?" Matt offered. "There might be some kinda drug in the bottle."

"Well if there is, it's all out now," Rick said. "And we've all been breathin' it."

Our little grotto fell utterly silent as we all considered what happened. The birds, even, seemed to have abandoned the place; and the creek had restrained its trickling into a hushed gurgle. Far off, as if echoing from a distant drive-in theatre, we heard the school bell announcing the end of another day. Our classmates were rushing down crowded hallways, grabbing skateboards, tossing books into lockers and straining toward the beckoning afternoon sunshine. Members of the swim team were stripping down for practice, and the ball players, the pride of Danville Middle School, were lacing up their cleats and pulling the visors of their caps down tight over their eyes.

"Let's just go, huh?" Rick said. "Everyone's goin' to the lake."

We looked around at each other. Matt shrugged his shoulders and that small gesture sealed our afternoon fate. Off to Lake Swansen we went, excitedly talking about how far we were going to dive, and the distance we were going to jump off the rope swing, and whether or not the Dodgers were going to disappoint us again this year.

At the top of the embankment I paused and looked back. There, in the shadows, was there a tiny pair of green eyes blinking at me? I waved, and though I'll not admit it, I could swear I saw a little hand wave back. A soft breeze carried the sound of bells to my ears.

"C'mon Darren," Daniel called out.

"Yeah, I'm comin'." After a last glance back I ran off to lose myself once again in the blissful magic of summertime fantasy.

ANDREW KICKING HORSE

ONE LIFER'S JOURNEY

REFLECTING ON these past twenty-three years of confinement, I have viewed, experienced, and been present to what can only be described as a miasmic swamp of lust, greed, hatred, fear, prejudice, and ignorance. To the solid citizen or pillar of society, it is no man's land, lighted occasionally by a sudden flare of publicity, then shrouded again in mystery. But to one who is himself an insignificant detail in its austere pattern, it exposes a thousand other facets: It is prison.

In the majority of institutions today, these concrete walls are basic storage bins for society of failed human potential and offer no "rehabilitation" despite this noun being a part of the State Department's luxurious name. A sanctuary for birds whose wings of freedom have been nipped or a ranch where all the sheep have been labeled black.

Although I must concede that at this institution I am currently housed at there is a ray of hope for those who choose to walk a different path in life and be able to reach out to others with compassion, humility, and genuine concern for one another despite race, creed, or color.

I arrived on Facility "A" back in 2007 from another facility at this same institution where I was one of the original six lifer mentors that started the S.A.P. Program on D-Yard. The program eventually was dismantled, mainly because of internal problems with the State and employees. I enjoyed this invaluable program immensely and have seen first hand the changes people can make if given the opportunity and means to change. When I first arrived here on A-Yard, I could not comprehend the various extracurricular programs being offered or even the amount of programs daily. It was exciting to be able to attend a poetry class or beading class, maybe getting involved with the A.I.C. painting project or simply toss horse shoes on the yard.

I watched as people of every ethnic background would be socializing in every aspect from sports to religious studies to different activities being offered, but more amazing, getting along with each other. This definitely was not like a "level four" setting I had ever been at. It was a project setting entitled the "Honor Yard" where you can partake in programs and grow as a human being and take responsibility for your actions and behavior.

Unfortunately, within what seems to be the last six months or so, there has been an influx of people, both staff and inmates, being housed or employed with hidden agendas and motives to destroy this atmosphere and program. Especially some of the correctional staff seems intent on provocation and destruction here. Just the other day, I overheard a staff cook conversing with new correctional staff, down-grading and belittling the program openly. It is exactly this clandestine unprofessional behavior by staff and hidden agendas by those residents housed here that will ultimately destroy this program. Then the ultimate, immutable description of this can be appropriately crammed into one potentous word: prison, a catacomb of dead hours and buried days. To those like myself who strive for humanity and peace, it will be remembered for what it was and should have continued to be.

BLANNON M. DUBOSE SR.

SADNESS, HATRED, AGONY

How can we even begin to write of joy, peace, love, pleasure
when there is so much dismay within my immediate surrounds
and beyond these gray, grim, prison walls.
How can I even commence to contemplate over
"correction," of tranquility, harmony
in a human society when all we see thoughout our entire life
is deceit, hardships, hypocrisy, deprivation, alienation,
annihilation, racism, ignorance, hatred, only to name a few.
How could we even speak of love in a world that knows
and practices hatred in its lowest and rawest form.
How can we even elaborate on the issue of harmony of all people
when just the mere complexion of my skin still causes people
to want to kill, mistreat and distrust me?
We all know this harmony amongst all people is obscure.
Don't take what is written as a form of abdication ... or frustration,
on the contrary, analyzing the "isms," hitherto,
in spite of all the bull I'm constantly confronted with.
Now, you want to talk about joy, peace, love and pleasure?

BLANNON M. DuBOSE SR.

VIOLENCE
OUTSIDE-IN + INSIDE-OUT

Prison is a microcosm of society
in its most deplorable existence.
Therefore prison is centered around repressive conditions
which lead to violence on any and all levels.
The hitherto is this,
a person in prison has death hovering over him on any given day
due to the fact of his/her very incarceration
in a State Prison.
Therefore, it would be fair to say that death
in prison
is ultimate expression of the violence,
the convict code of honor,
or respect.
What grew out of this form of unhappiness and misery
of filth and external decay
of prison life
is no human being per se,
but deplorable results of
deplorable laws.
This is a reality too.
Another form of violence,
as you know,
is psychological abuse
in all of its pervasive forms.
It affects everything done,
every decision.
Even those who want to stay out of trouble

are deeply effected,
Often to immobility over measuring every little detail
of an interaction: a glance,
a new routine, a letter,
a day, a week or two late,
a refused appointment,
a comment about the mail.
Every small encounter may have multiple meanings
and serious disciplinary repercussions.
This happening to individuals daily.
They react in a violent manner,
verbally or physically
because of a new routine,
it's madness.
I know you're wondering why I'm bringing all this
to your attention
For various reasons—For one,
I don't want you to be misled,
but to only be enlightened
of imprisonment and what it does to a person.
I was susceptible on both accounts.
Yes, they're degrading and debasing forms
of lifestyles, but still why tell you?
It's quite obvious:
I'm trying to get you to understand my situation,
not sympathize with it.

UNREALISTIC EXPECTATIONS

She expects much from a man that only can give what he has,
and what he has is all that he as a man is capable of giving.
In her mind she accuses him of being selfish and unfair,
but what she does not understand but does realize is that,
she does not give all that she is capable of giving.
She's consciously attempting to manipulate her will onto him,
because she is a very insecure individual.
So in an attempt to ease her mind,
she attempts to confuse and distort him.
In her unbalanced mind, the more he resist
the deeper her anger goes.
Her mind is filled with words
she'll use in another attempt
to create her guilt in him.
Howbeit, he's a strong man in mind,
again escaping her insecurity.
She does not realize that she's been taught and conditioned to be
as she is!
She does not realize that her pain is her own,
by her own.
She must understand that the perfect image in her mind
is only what she thinks she wants,
that the, image will
always remain elusive,
even if he were to comply with her insecurities.
When she demands such unrealistic expectations,
to the degree and extent that she does,
she negates her own womanness,
she becomes her own self-destruction.

BLANNON M. DuBOSE SR.

BEAUTIFUL REALITY

Beautiful reality is what you are
and not what society assumes it to be.
When you look at your own beauty,
you must assess that beauty with your own mind's eye.
To see and understand the essence
of your own individual beauty,
you must eliminate
the mind's thoughts that society conditions us to manifest
within the depth of our mind.
In a society where we place physical beauty
above all else,
we slowly lose the true essence of that
which is most beautiful—
Beauty of character.

DANIEL WHILTON

ESCAPE

The last things I ever saw
Were the slices of a waxing moon.
Deep in your eyes of charity,
And brimming with wonder,
You laughed and tossed your hair—
Silver plumage shining with stars,
Broken by the final sigh of what we had earned,

So abruptly it stopped
And threw me from your arms,
And the tears poured from my eyes.
Delicate paper ghosts in black silk,
Ordinary, plain and beautiful,
Lift my chin with opal fingers.
Awakened by the first drops of rain,
The wind through your feathers —
brings silence —
flying —
night.

DANIEL WHILTON

MISTAKES?

V

The errors we make will bind our hands and crush our tender heels
Will tell us that they understand but won't know how it feels
And the eyeless ghouls of yesterday will taint our every smile
By haunting us with regretted past, Ambrosia turned to bile

V

We can say what we want to but it'll never change a thing
Our histories are immortal wasps that never lose their sting
We commiserate for those who died, funeral tears we've shed
Conscious of this fleeting joke, lost count of times we've bled

V

Don't pray for us but don't forget these words, because they're true
We admit we're fools, saturnine, the proud, sardonic few
Our memories are sacrosanct, forever living free
From the chains of past mistakes, our defunct vacuity

C

It's always the things we couldn't see
What we wished we could've had or wanted to achieve
We suffer for living aggressively
But we'll suffer more if we live in fear of failure and mortality.

DANIEL WHILTON

LYING IN THE ODIOUS

I'll never be awake long enough
to hear your baited breathing.
Your late-night sobbing does not puncture
this fur-mantled, endless sleep.
Neither day nor night can influence
my heavy lids to open and see
the imperfect and unresolved conditions
that have saturated me.

I'd much rather stay hidden and lonesome.
I ache but it's who I am.
I choose to do only that which I know.
I fear that new things will change us.
How would I know if you care for me?
I can't take this risk—
I've been left with your breath and Perditional smile
inside of my freshly dug grave.

I try very hard to be proud of myself
and I always say the right things.
But too many hours here on this bed
has scarred my back with pain.
So if I'm forced to make weary decisions—
I think I'll just kill myself now.
I'd rather sleep for Eternity
than wake up and realize you're gone.

If you would only wake up to me;
If you would only please talk to me;
If you would only be the one to see the end has come and it's over.

Pathetic dreams are the ones we recall.
We hide from the sun when the moon starts to fall.
Beaten by victims of squalor and hate,
the chances we've missed start to resonate.
Disharmony breeds a startling light
where shadows and spectres show putrescence bright.
Look in my eyes and you'll see what I mean—
sleep well and quiet, my angel.

DANIEL WHILTON

SOME KINDS

I'm an old man
It's a lonely feeling —being pale and dark on an empty road
Knowing the world is warm and made of fire—
                                    Bathed in the sun's light
Knowing the world gave me a shot and I missed.

I'm a stupid man
It's been done a lot —"It's not over yet"— I scream and shout
I'm out of time and money
I'll just sit down and shut up.

I'm an old man.

DANIEL WHILTON

SUCH A CLEVER BOY

How, in the Creator's name, am I going to ascend?
The fire's been licking the balls of my feet for some time now.
Black soil has pitted my porous flesh during every transgression.
This obsession is too far gone to pull it back.
Darkness is cliche but it's what I feel.
I'm not jaded enough to call it emptiness—no, that's a lie.
I'm not jagged or broken but I cut and break everything I touch,
like Midas.
I'm Brutus.
The audacity I wield like a club is ridiculous.
I've been destined to descend since my fangs were formed.
Darkness is just part of it, I'm falling and falling.
The falling doesn't worry me, it's my arrival at the bottom.
The light has enticed my benevolent eye with silver and peace.
The flames burned the pain of sight and hope from the other.
I've come full circle, sucking my thumb and expecting nothing.
How will I be seen in history?
With very little time to ponder that, I rush away—no, scurry away
to nibble at a crumb, a morsel of moldy and uninspired cheese,
savoring the taste, vomiting from within.

I fell from heaven and landed in hell, so predictable, but
where else would I go? I've no home, I've no soul; I sold it for more
cheese, what else?
I maintain that I do not stand stoic and alone in this world.

Some day I'll see the truth but until then I'll rely on my
    passionate illusions.
I am dark and empty, I am a piece of cheese,
moldy and dramatic, sometimes ridiculous, but never bored.
Ah ... finally the bottom ...

DANIEL WHILTON

MY WASTELAND

I haven't done anything right.
I've sat here and decayed.
I'm lost and have been for so long.
I've finally fallen through the ice.
The me I am slew the me I knew.
I can't look in the mirror.
Sometimes I am consumed by bloodlust,
something intense and heroic.
I am worthless; it costs nothing to die—
I'm a dollar to a millionaire.
The lower half is frozen, dead.
The upper half is helpless, bled.
Welcome to my wasteland, it's real.
It's where I go when I'm alive;
it's where I'll go when I die.
It's my final broken, shattered home.

DANIEL WHILTON

I'M DONE

Suicide always seemed wrong,
surrounded by the ocean air—
From a distance it held my eyes (nothing menacing).
Utopian beauty that triggered tears.
I never knew what it was, really.
Maybe a castle with kings and knights,
royal plumage in the wind: Dark eyes, burning bright.
Stone halls rich with age, tapestries adorning barren space.
Perhaps a city with flying cars, or talking fish—
something fantastic and breathtaking.
Like a weapons plant building the big one,
a new fascination, a ready-to-eat thrill (another world with
    time to kill).

It's a prison, it's a jail,
it's a waiting room for those who've failed.
I have my tools here with me, my things,
just enough to deafen, for me, pain sings.
I was betrayed, was accused,
and found lying on the kitchen floor (bleeding out).
I'm alone, done, afraid of my fears—
the circus left town, caged, I left with them.

My eyes are shut, as is my mouth; my foolish heart is dead.
My crotch is empty, 133 days spent clean, I've bled.
It's the only release I could have felt, the only one I know.
I'm mislabelled, I'm not alone, I can't run, I'm done.

DORTELL WILLIAMS

SEEKING REDEMPTION IN THE CURSE
OF RETRIBUTION

A vast sea of brown, black and poor white faces
locked away, incarcerated, incapacitated.

Underrepresented minorities in the bigger world,
yet, overflowing and populous castaways.

Mother earth desires to kiss every potential prince,
but too often the cruel
circumstances of life kiss them first;
and like biblical Egypt,
the world is plagued with frogs.

The earth's heartbeat still palpitates
beneath her black, brown and white surface.
She weeps tears of joy by way
of rain for the taste of justice;
and like a woman scorned,
she floods with rivulets at injustice.

Countless hordes of forlorn souls
carelessly hurled into no man's land.
Many drank the water of life,
but from the most bitter of wells.
Wells of poverty and prejudice,
marginalization and miseducation.

Fortune missed, luck escaped, men and women
who once had their whole lives to live and lead;

now reduced to letting others define them,
and write their stories for them—their way.

All the majestic places in the world, the Sendero
Luminosos (Peru), Dgannsk (Poland), Ruwenzori (Uganda),
couldn't find their way into the prisoner mindset,
only the confines of their ghettoes,
barrios and decrepit reservations.

Knocked to and fro by the storms of circumstance,
enveloped by failure, rich in misfortune
and deluged by game-losing fumbles.

They became trapped monsters
trapped within themselves, and now...
they are trapped among each other;
their destitution and deprivation compounded.

In prison the winds blow in every direction at once,
intense peer pressure from elements of the underworld,
abuse from misery-loving, sadistic guards.

Time eludes prison; minds stay stuck
in old memories, styles and technology.
The joint sets you back a hundred
years behind the modern world.

Primitive, depriving, idle;
sapping the soul,
spawning the psychotic.
Everyone, even the guards,
dwell in their own darkness.

Young men convalesced on stained mattresses, cookie-
sheet thin, by unadulterated and forced mindlessness.

Old men reserved by imposed inactivity
and depressed bouts of sleep.

Tamed into unproductivity and
dependency by relentless punishment;
prisoners are the politicians' ascension souvenirs.

Generous and giving,
the earth groans at all the deprivation.
2.2 million souls caged
and fastooned to failure.

Opportunities for redemption are sparse
and rare—like a commodity.
Penitence, "correction" and
rehabilitation are misnomers.

So the world changes, grows and matures,
but prisoners are chained to retardation.

Seeds grow into plants, cocoons to butterflies;
eggs break into fowls, pups into K-9s.

In prison, under the punishment model,
every dawn is the same,
no celestial orange or violet
streaks painted across the sky,
and men's hearts don't change;
there's nothing to soften
the hard lives that led to stone hearts.

Redemption is like a water reflection in a small pond,
only big enough to see one's own private duplication.

Infected by misrule, wretchedness and deep angst,
some still strive for the revival
of inherent good within all.

Others are reluctant to cross
the frontiers of inner-change,
full aware of the challenge,
magnified by societal neglect.

The redeeming sun hides its countenance
from these forlorn men and women.

These are deprived of the elixirs
that could reform potential productive minds.
The warehouse model
mercilessly fetters them to shadiness.

Yet the majority are pilgrims,
 just passing though this
wilderness of god-forsaken concrete and steel.

Waiting for the day of release, transporting,
like a homicidal contagion, the corruption of
Brienne, Goshen and fallen Megiddo.

DORTELL WILLIAMS

NO ONE WOULD UNDERSTAND

What if you could catch the light blue air and hold it in hand?

Caress the texture of ether— a puffy cloud; made a thousand stone's throws from land.

Breathe the water like a tropical fish—striped, yellow and green; and ocean's waving floor made of golden sand.

Change by metamorphosis like a motley chameleon, melding so magnificently into the pliant land.

To harness the luminous spectrum, a sight unseen, a feat unfathomable; and light years from bland.

Wrestle with electricity, as it glows like flourescent against your melanin tan.

What if you could perform, amazing like so . . . even if you could, no one would understand.

DORTELL WILLIAMS

YOU'RE POOR AND IN PRISON

YOU'RE ARRESTED. You've committed some crime—or maybe you didn't. You say you didn't, but the fact is ... you're in jail. The evidence amounts to mere accusations; nothing physical to link you to the crime. Nevertheless, it's the establishment that has the power, and they're respected and you're not. You are the accused. You're poor, and even if you're not, lawyers cost a fortune.

You don't have a record, but there's a history of wrong doing by the system. No one seems to care. You were voiceless in society and you'll be voiceless in jail.

In court your hand-me-down threads, your pigmented skin, and your penury work feverishly against you behind the scenes. Your court-appointed attorney tramples in looking tired, he's overworked. He immediately explains that his caseload is overflowing—even before he tells you the specifics of your case. He doesn't introduce himself. He never asks your version of the events. The case is postponed the court docket is in arrears.

It's back to the Los Angeles County Jail until the next date, some thirty to sixty days ahead. The conditions in the county jail are horrendous. The joint is overcrowded, tension simmers just under a boil. Staph infections and other communicables are epidemic. Like you, most of your new peers are in for minor crimes, but they're stuck because they can't make bail. Many are coerced by over burdened attorneys—like yours—to plead out. The jail conditions are so atrocious most likely will. It's by design. It keeps an over-taxed system from otherwise certain congestion and meltdown.

You're hauled off to the holding cages in the rear of the court, out of sight from the public. Your worried family attempts to wave, but you're whisked off too quickly by the guards. You find yourself being unexpectedly sentenced soon after the next hearing, where the judge alters your fate by over a decade.

"It was a misdemeanor," you plead. Then you remember all those pro-prison initiatives the establishment scared you into voting for. Your anxiety is oddly calmed by the realization that this is a pro-prison culture. It is a fact you now face readily, only because you see the other side of it. The judge asserts a disclaimer for the record. He disagrees with the sentence, but his hands are tied: mandatory sentencing statutes. He has no choice.

The judge advises you of your right to appeal. But it is a futile right. You know it, he knows it. Everything is political, even justice. He must maintain a tough-on-crime record to advance his career. The appellate judges are no different. The system is run by perception, not justice.

You're in prison now—banished, cast away; you feel thrown away. You think about how you were denied grants and loans for higher education, but now the system is eager to spend upwards of $40,000 a year to keep you shelved and idle.

You daydream about all the things you could be doing with $40,000 bucks. You could be out on bail with change to spare. You could feast yourself on a nice meal to quell those nagging hunger pangs. Instead, your new prison peers are feasting their eyes on you.

The guards treat you like cattle, rudely ushering you here, callously prodding you there. The prisoners and guards mean-mug you for an introduction. The guards finally toss you into the general population; into a nether world filed to the brim with others, yet a feverish loneliness engulfs your desolate soul.

Though still overcrowded, the big house is more spacious than the dilapidated county jail. That, too, is by design. It's part of the lure to coax you to move on from the county.

The grounds are massive and the compound is cleaner. It should be—most of the state prisons are much newer than the state's universities that have been neglected for over two decades. California's priority seems to be to incarcerate, not educate.

In the housing unit there's a small cell waiting anxiously for a warm body like yours. There's another man in there you'll probably spend the majority of your conscious and unconscious hours with, crammed within a space the size of your average closet for twenty-three hours a day. Society calls this space a cell—it looks more like a cage to you. Semantics? You don't think so.

During orientation the guards tell you to act civilized, though they treat you rather savagely.

They feed you three times a day, yet you're hungry all the time. The food is tasteless, and has textures you've never experienced before. It's not a good thing!

You get a concrete roof over your crawl space, or what could very well become your tomb. You get a change of clothes every week and a small space for exercise every now and then. Yet it's not all it's billed up to be. It is certainly not the resort-type living you've heard so much about.

Taxpayers pay for everything anyway. At least that's the prevailing myth. The prison does provide tooth paste, though it's powdered, and when available. There's also soap, though it's generic, and makes you itch like you've been rolling around in the grass. Otherwise you're on your own.

If you're one of the more fortunate ones you'll be assigned a job with pay. As a porter or yard crew worker you could earn 8 cents an hour. It will help subsidize your $5.00 medical copayment. Actually, it's better to just not get sick. Then you can use the money for copies required for your futile appeal, 10 to 12 cents, depending on who you ask. But don't fret, if you're a little short they'll just put a hold on your account for the amount due and tax your next pay period religiously.

You wish you could vote, but you can't. However, you're still a very important part of the political system. You see, whatever political district you happen to be housed in will count you as part of the civilian population, though you get no benefits for it whatsoever: It's three-fifths of a person all over again.

Still, you won't be totally forgotten by the politicians.

Though they won't represent you, they'll certainly tell the public about you. Though you're nonviolent, you'll be lumped in with the "worst of the worst": murderers, rapists and child molesters. What they won't tell the public is that the majority of offenders are in for some drug-related crime that stem from the worn out and failed war on drugs.

The politicians don't tell the public that the vast majority of prisoners are non-violent, and that most violent offenders -- particularly lifers -- cause very few, if any, problems. It's the bad apples, like anywhere else in life, who cause most of the trouble.

The demagogues will use you as fodder to fulfill their political aspirations. And they'll line the pockets of prison industry moguls with new and lucrative construction projects. They've built thirty-two new prisons in the last two decades -- and $15 billion is slated for more.

When you are finally allowed to call home, you're amazed to find the rates for your calls are through the roof. The phone companies use an animated voice to tell you it's $3.00 just to connect and 89 cents per minute thereafter. They probably don't use live people because they wouldn't be able to hold a straight face.

You find it hard to sleep at night because the light doesn't go all the way out. And the guards take inventory of you some five times during the night; keys jingling, communications radio blaring, shattering the silence.

You marvel that everything is expected of you, but nothing is invested in you. You're amazed at the level of demands placed on you by your keepers, yet they barely lift a finger to serve as an example. You have to be "blue or bleeding" to have an illness validated to get time off from work. Yet your keepers have the highest sick-time abuse record of all law enforcement agencies.

You're expected to be at your job assignment promptly each and every day for the rest of your life sentence, yet you often have to wait on them to arrive to get started. There's a constant and consistent hypocrisy that pervades the place, yet you don't rack your brains trying to figure it out.

You know many of the guards come from some of the same neighborhoods and niches of America you did. They're only required to have a **GED** or high school diploma to be employed. However, earning $80,000-plus with overtime, they are in a tax bracket that exceeds anything they ever dreamed of and supersedes anything you've ever come close to. So they sport an attitude like it's part of their uniform. They treat you like a Negro in the Jim Crow Confederate South -- no matter what race you are. It's about class, not race they say. Yet race and class seem to converge such that they echo the same social pictures once drawn solely by race. The truth is, you're in prison, not so much for what you did, but for the zip code you claimed; or the lack of digits on your paycheck, if you even earned one.

It's for these reasons you're in prison and—for a while at least— this is where you'll be.

DORTELL WILLIAMS

ANIMATION FOR THE CHARACTERS
BEHIND BARS

PRISONERS CAN be a lively set of characters—animated souls who express themselves in a variety of entertaining ways: chatting, gossiping, joking, gesturing, challenging and competing. Then we have the more ominous expressions: the mad-dog stares, the bravado struts and the myriad violence. Thanks to Vita Rabinovich, add to that animation as an expression of art.

At five feet in stature, she is clearly the smallest creature in the classroom. Yet she commands a subtle and steadfast respect among her enthusiastic class of eight. They listen attentively as she recites the jargon of her art, explaining sequences, scenes and action columns. Pencil in hand, I sit quietly as a quest to watch and record. Rabinovich patiently describes the use of pixels, overlapping actions and picture design so smoothly that even an onlooker is able to quickly grasp the concepts.

The volunteer group eagerly awaits each weekly, four hour class to learn a more productive, non-injurious type of shooting. Rabinovich, a young, rosy-cheeked college student, who wears her sandy-blonde hair tied and tucked behind her head, explains shots of 1s or 2s for one-second animation with either 12 or 24 frames; along with other nuances of the trade, such as angles and sound. The classmates are jovial, trading verbal slams and tossing punchlines in between each lesson. We all smile and chuckle at some of the banter, including Rabinovich; and when it gets out of hand a simple, "Come on guys," is enough to restore order.

The challenge in teaching these men isn't struggling to get them to behave, but rather not being allowed to bring cameras and computers into this maximum-security setting to make the final product.

So she takes their work with her and completes it offsite, shooting it, downloading the shots and sequencing the frames. In the end, there is an amazing array of art transformed from motionless sketches to invigorating, colorful animation.

It's nothing short of impressive.

Some of the work is to be featured at www.giantelephants.com, The website of Giant Elephants Roam, a non-profit group that introduces animation education to prisons, and, after a few short weeks, brings refreshing, animated films out. Ultimately, they are working to spread the art, reform the men and generate a new interest in animation inside and out.

The fellas share a deeper camaraderie in the seclusion of a classroom than is possible on the yard, where the mask of prison is prevalent, and prisoners are generally more distant with their emotions. On the yard, the telling of war stories eat away at untold hours from one group to the next, each more wild and dramatic than the first time told. In the classroom emotions are shared deeper than ever, and the guys are more open to their frailties. On the yard, the spirit of competition rules in sports, exercise and occasional clashes. In the classroom, a subtle collaboration presides and the men work together to create alluring art.

John Hernandez (the prisoners' names have been changed), a salt- and pepper-haired screenwriter serving life without the possibility of parole for murder, relates the class to his budding comic art. An intelligent, studious man, Hernadez is serious about gaining all he can from this class.

Robert Tilton, a phenomenal painter featured last year in the Antelope Valley Press, and also in for murder, enjoys the class for what it adds to his painting skills. "I believe art opens the mind," he tells me during break. Tilton has been locked up for 26 years and believes this class is an opportunity of a life time.

Rabinovich scans the room with her deep sea-biue eyes for a hand to pick in response to her question. Frank O'Neal, another talented painter, answers correctly, as is usual among this gifted group. O'Neal says the class is therapeutic and gives him something positive to do, rather than flailing in the abundance of non-productive activities prison offers. Indeed, it is a shame that men must rust in the concrete catacombs of state warehouses, when empty brains could be filled with constructive and productive, life-changing knowledge.

Rabinovich has a subtle way of infusing life's lessons in her teachings of animation. She emphasizes working together, and the importance of collaboration in production. "Sometimes you have to compromise your work for the group, you have to listen to details and communicate," she teaches. A few of the men are politely transfixed on her lecture, while others diligently take notes. I do the same.

"Planning is everything, guys, and your timing must be right and purposeful, " she stresses. Her lessons are universal.

With her teaching, Rabinovich sparks a redeeming element in these men—men whose past self-centered ways, perhaps, brought them here. Now they learn the bigger picture: About a world that operates by the mores of patience, sharing and compromise, learning not only to be responsible for themselves, but also for one another. Her approach is undeniably effective. These are men I have shared space with for years and Rabinovich has given us all a new perspective.

A burly correctional officer checks in periodically, decked with myriad equipment and weapons: a mace canister, a baton, a flashlight and a ready alarm to summon his comrades at the slightest hint of a threat.

Yet, with the delicate chisel of art, instilling values and subtly explaining etiquette, Rabinovich prunes the hardness off these mens' hearts with each lesson—a feat no gun, mace canister, baton or weaponized flashlight could ever do.

DORTELL WILLIAMS

IS ANYONE WORTHLESS?

In a way, it was kind of like the Rich Man and Lazarus story from the Bible. The rich man lived a life of selfish, apathetic abundance, while humble Lazarus subsisted in a life of want and need.

When the rich man found himself in the sphere of hell at the end of life's bling-bling journey, he worried about his remaining five brothers from this life. He wished he could somehow cross the great gulf between eternal damnation and the present to warn his beloved kin, but the gulf was insurmountable.

Prison is like that hell, a terrestrial hades of eternal discomfort, suffering and damnation for lifers. Only, with the guidance of people like Susan Zaks, that great gulf can be breached and our beloved can be warned.

Zaks is program coordinator of Try Again, a crime prevention program developed in 1997; formally named Project Teen Reach. Zaks, and a number of others, ferry troubled youth deep within the gates of this hell so they can hear what it's like inside the dark entrails of the beast.

The kids range from fourteen to eighteen years of age, and are already within the court's purview. Charged with everything from joy riding to burglary and vandalism, they are processed in like inmates, and then, like a more gentler Scared Straight program, warned, admonished and sermonized—in-your-face-style—by real, live convicts.

"I hope you left your attitudes outside because this is our house. Your gang-crew or crime won't impress us, it has all been done before. I got scars and tattoos older than all of you," said Hucjo Machuca, a life prisoner and member of Convicts Reaching Out to People (or CROP).

"What you need to do," Machuca continues, "is listen to what we have to say, and if anything sounds familiar from our stories, you need to use that critical thinking process. Otherwise you will find yourself in a cell right next to mine." The kids were silent and listening intensely; they didn't budge.

CROP is a successful, eight year intervention group of caring incarcerated men—mostly lifers—who desire a better life for the next at-risk generation. They hate to see any more thrown away. They practice peer-education, self-study and participate in any number of educational activities they can manage to pull within the walls here at the State Prison in Los Angeles County.

Many of these dedicated men may never see the streets again, yet opportunities to educate themselve, and mentor the majority of others who will be released, give them purpose and make them valuable—a commodity, inside and outside.

Their effectiveness and example makes for a poignant lesson, not only for troubled youth, but also for a society that believes they're worthless, incorrigible and don't deserve even the dignity to learn and educate themselves. I suppose everyone has worth after all.

MARTEZ DYER

ORWELL SPEAKS!!!

LANGUAGE IS DEAD!
Hung by velvet rope
Broken tender neck of speech
on deaf ears fell

OPINION IS DEAD!
Murdered by methods unconventional
politically correctly sacrificed
drained and void of value

LANGUAGE IS ALIVE!
In the crawl spaces of memory only
Forgotten in fear
alongside identity buried

THE INDIVIDUAL IS DEAD!
Between ideas
few distinctions made
Impossible now to pick your shadow from a lineup

VOICES MERE RIPPLES IN A SEA OF ECHOES
UNHEARD AND REMEMBERED VAGUELY . . .

RELIGION IS DEATH!
Pagan parasites feasting on indecision
baring of teeth/drawing of blood

FREEDOM IS DEAD!
Liberty—a palm across face
Justice—salt in the wounds of innocence
Equality—a collage of "I can" and "You can'ts"

FREE WILL IS DEAD!
Behind veil of passivity
Humanity hides

A "RIGHT" IS NOW A PRIVILEGE
BY CONSENSUS!!!!

MARTEZ DYER

SWARM OF SILENCE

SILENCE
     hear me whisper,
piercing your shield
  with the sharpened tip of sound.
SILENCE
     hear me scream
shattering the mute reflections of quiet.
SILENCE
     hear me roar;
an unsettling crescendo,
  like a dull blade across throat of stillness.
SILENCE
     hear the words
of one unafraid to mouth them;
  hear my voice,
an anthem of echoes
       piggybacking thin air.
Hear the noise
  of a thousand daggers
riding the waves of vibration
  through the heart of a silent storm.
Embracing nudity of speech
  reading lips of language . . .

Insufferable Peace
  befallen mime-like reality;
with so much to say
     it's hard to hear—SILENCE

Only in Death
   will I succumb,
a reluctant surrender buried
            with remnants of SOUND.

MARTEZ DYER

THE ARRIVALS
FOR THOSE WHO CHOOSE TO BELIEVE

I.

The falling of the skies
into the oceans drowned
the ascension of the ground
above the heavens rise

II.

The sinking of the Sun
below the surface crawl
in preparation for the one
who prophesized it all

III.

The running out of time
the taste of fruit forbidden
fresh footsteps across the mind
memories of what was written

IV.

The remains of what was once before
fragments of past left behind
along the way souls in scores
unable to forge their place in line

V.

The taking of a moment
to breathe in what's been done

the making of atonement
to he who has come

      He who has come.

MARTEZ DYER

ON DEAF EARS FELL
[PRISON SONG]

As mine hands meet
      each to each in prayer
and mine words have mustered
      courage to soar . . .

As mine knees buckle
      before bed in which I wish to lie
and mine eyes deny
      tears wish to cry . . .

As mine heart beats
      a steady pulse in the mute of night
and mine blood a fluid whisper
      through corridors of crowded arteries

I IMAGINE THAT SOMEONE SOMEWHERE HEARS

As mine breath slows
      to shadow's pace
and mine faith hovers
      overhead this blackened tomb . . .

As mine lips seal themselves
      and the barrage of words
just behind them subdued . . .

As mine hope withers
       like a dream to an awakening
and mine despair fed
       by silky sighs of quiet

I CONTEND THAT NO ONE NOTHING ANYWHERE HEARS . . .

Silence speaks to no one who listens.

HUGO MACHUCA

TO ATONE

California State Prison-Los Angeles at Lancaster
CROP (Convicts Reaching Out to People)

FOR ME it always starts the same way: with a knot in my stomach in anticipation of welcoming another group of at-risk youth to our diversion program. Will we plant a seed in any one of these youngsters? Can they understand the system that doesn't care about age anymore? It involves billions of dollars and is one of California's biggest industries.

Maybe a few can grasp it, but that problem has to compete with Pop's beatings, or no father, only a mother strung out on crack or too busy to worry about the child she gave life to. That's what CROP has to compete with when we focus on gangs, drugs, choices, respect, responsibility and prison life. But this is a challenge we seek when these youngsters come to the prison. We sincerely hope that in reaching out to youth we can atone for the lives we have taken and the damage we have caused our communities.

The healing is not only for our victims but for ourselves. This is something that crept up on us without knowing. Through searching our lives for that wrong choice and trauma that occurred early in our lives and set us on a destructive road to prison, we found empathy for our victims and self esteem, even though some will never see freedom again.

Eight years ago, 25 men came together to form the foundation of CROP. My journey to CROP began 14 years earlier at a prison known throughout the system as the "Gladiator School": Deuel Vocational Institution in Tracy California. It was 1986 and I was in administrative segregation, accused of a violent act. During my stay in Ad-Seg, I had an attitude toward the guards. This earned me a cell on a mixed tier in K wing. The reason it's called mixed tier: Normally if you're from Southern or Northern California, or from a certain prison, you are separated by a tier. Because of my behavior towards the guards, they put me on a tier that had more enemies than friends.

One day I was caught off guard and was speared through the cell bars as I was walking to the shower. I was taken to San Juaquin Hospital, where they performed exploratory surgery to repair the damage caused by the prison-made spear. During my week in the hospital, I laid on my back handcuffed to the bed and was given a shot of morphine whenever I complained of pain due to the scar I had from my chest to my lower abdomen. This nurse would nervously enter my room with wide, cautious eyes to perform her duties.

Even with the morphine-induced haze, her cautious behavior bothered me, but because of the morphine, I couldn't figure out why it continued to bother me. When I was sent back to the prison, the morphine wore off and some clarity began to set in.

That nurse's fear of me at the hospital was a catalyst for that very important conversation every man has with himself. I was 24 years old, in prison for second degree murder. Shaved head, bench pressing 300 lbs and a gruff look. My internal conversation began with a few questions: Am I really a thug at heart? Does everything about me give that thuggish vibe to the world? I took the life of a mother's son. Why haven't I spent any time thinking about that?

Answering the first question was uncomplicated and surprising. At my core, I was not a thug or a gangster. There was the love and tenderness my mother and three sisters always gave me, even when I was disrespectful of them. My sister Gia was the most emotional and traumatic of my three sisters. But once when the Rampart crash police rounded up a few *cholos*, meaning to beat them down and drop us off in our rival's territory, Gia parked her car, asked the cops questions, and when the answers were not to her satisfaction, she asked to follow them. They refused, and told her to leave or be arrested. She challenged them to arrest her, and when they wouldn't she spit in one's face. So instead of the beat down for the *cholos,* we went to Rampart Station.

Today, during our CROP presentation, I want to plant this seed:

Regardless of the serious problems you face in your young lives—violence at home or in the streets, drugs, etc.—don't internalize the issue. The fact that you have to deal with these problems does not mean you are a bad person who deserves these problems. But the choices you make during this time in your young lives will determine the road you end up on. If you see similariites in CROP members life stories, then you need to use that critical thinking process the creator gave you.

I don't believe this is the future for any one of you. Many people do believe prison is your future. Prove them wrong. Take control of your life. Challenge the adults that brought you here. Tell them you want to get out of the gang life or drugs. Whatever issues you have, ask them for help and I promise you they will help or they will direct you to someone who will. Remember, a sign of intelligence is the ability to ask for help!

NOTE: THE CROP PROGRAM WAS CREATED BY CONVICTS BEFORE THE HONOR YARD WAS ESTABLISHED, AND IT WAS SUPPORTED AND SPONSORED BY FREE STAFF AND CORRECTIONAL OFFICERS LIKE L. RAZO, RETIRED PAROLE AGENT DEAN CRENSHAW, AND OUR BIGGEST SUPPORTER, SERGEANT D. TIDWELL.

DUNCAN MARTINEZ

THE WONDER OF LIFE

CRACKED CONCRETE and dismal lighting gave no life to a room full of lost lives, men ravaged by the truth of consequences. The dying grey and hard edges spoke to and demanded a callous regard in every way; a place of despair and ultimately, a place of the dead. Cells about a room of metal tables, metal stools welded in place about them. Soft was not allowed, from the place or the men trapped inside. A grim nothing almost perfectly spartan in every way, by design and in design: a factory of spartan men. Dead men who had yet to die.

He was crying, sullen tears that swept from pain to pain in the imagined world in which he allowed his emotions to scream with raging tears, through them—primeval, visceral, real. The kind of scream that spoke to the soul and begged, begged for something more. Inside, though, all of it kept inside, held deep in a chasm of hate and despair—a place where there was nothing but, and that was the worst of it.

He smiled across the table. His eyes lacking excitement, for the gesture, the arching of lips, meant nothing. No one cared about the look, or the pain for that matter. At most, if they bothered to notice, they would have interpreted it as a form of weakness and felt contempt for it—acidic loathing. That was the way of this world, this place, a way beyond and without. He tried to grasp hold, to fit in, to understand. He tried to hide behind who and what he was, become another number, another spartan trapped in the grinding wheel of stoicism and hatred. He immersed himself in the here and now, in the place, eyes vigilant and indisposed, hands ready to make fists, and fury beneath every expression—fury was the only emotion allowed. He tried to find the sanctity of something or anything within the angst and turmoil that stewed about him, for he was surrounded by desperate men, men filled with insatiable need, a need that could be filled with things he could only regret. He had once believed that there could be more, that there had to be something, but the world he plodded through did not allow for dreams.

His smile, a dead thing he showed for an instant and let fade, was simple and without obvious concern. From this side of the table it was the height of expression, for that, too was the way of his world. The cards he held were marvelous, and he was smiling to his partner to tell him just that. He would bid it just so, and they would win the game. Likely or not, for it did not matter; there would be another game after this one, and then another. They would play these cards into submission and then start on another deck. They would do this again and again until something forced them to stop: an act of violence would be needed to bring back the calm. The calm that meant more cards and more hands, and—at best—useless smiles. And that was the extent of his emotions, a bleak smile that some would see as too much.

How it played out meant less, now that he had thought about it, not to the smile or the scream or the tears. He was giving what was required and nothing more because that was all there was to do—that was the way. He was not allowed anything else, for anything additional would have been a sign of weakness, and he knew how that road ended. When the spark of life is gone, the eyes begin to fade.

He wanted to scream, to let it all out, to say that this is not a life. That they deserved more, something more, a way to have real smiles; a way not to simply hate each other because that was all there was to do. He saw bitterness and cynicism, angst and uncaring, men lost to being spartans, soldiers for life with nothing but the readiness of same. I'll kill you if you cross me, jump on you if you look weak; I'll ruin you the way I was ruined because there is no other option. How could there be a world where there was nothing but pain?

He would remember, when he could handle it, a life before all this. Friends, now blank faces and anecdotes that flitted past occasionally. He did not remember the specifics—it was too alien to what he knew, what he had become. A sister, a loving and caring sister, they had been so close. . . . She did not visit anymore. It was too hard for both of them. She had succeeded and he, well, he had not. They had been friends, closer than close, the best of pals, and now she had everything and he . . . he had to suffer every day, hand after hand, every hour vigilant only to stay alive; but caring nothing for any of it. She knew the pain, and he had seen the knowledge in her eyes the last time she came. She understood the anguish that was his every minute, and that there was nothing in the world she could do to fix any of it. The powers that be were simply too happy to let any changes come, too stupid to see that all they were doing was making spartans that could never again come back to their streets, soldiers that knew nothing but.

She knew all of it, and when she had looked away to hide the tears, he saw that he was ruining her by association.

She told people he was dead. It was easier that way. He told people he had no family. They nodded, for many of them lived the same truth.

He screamed again, the echoes riding and deriding off his inner skull. He sulked as he played a jack, recoiling against everything as he watched the pile drift away. How do you express anything when expressing is dictated against? How do you give or release or grow, when everything is internal and —even then—at best barely allowed? How?

The men about him, cold and dismal in their approach, did everything so that nothing meant anything—carefully so. If you cared, you could be exploited. If you internalized, no one ever knew. It was simply too much, too grey, too bleak. He could not, simply, take it any more. Searching the room, searching for anything that might speak to him, speak of anything more than what he had and was. Even his memories had gone grey—fading into a wilderness of hate and despair that allowed for nothing. He knew the words, the litany of hope and the reprisals of same. He knew, without knowing, more than Sartre ever could. He knew . . . that he could not look at any of it anymore.

Looking away, his eyes found a window, a plastic thing broken years before by some unknown force. It was high up and dirty, and no one had ever cared enough to clean it. Through it, beyond it, was the sky and stars. He could make out one, just barely catching the flicker and glow through the morass of cracks and dirt. So distant, so old, it acted as inspiration for most: a thing of hope and desire, representing the totality of life and all that it could be. It was alive, for them, a thing of future, a guide to more, twinkling with the unknown— giving of itself all that was eternal.

But not for him. For him the star signified something beyond reach—all of the somethings beyond reach. It represented everything they had taken away, the loss of a life: his life, career, family, everything. It was the wiles and whims of a life unled, every twinkle a mockery of what he should have become. The thing that screamed and raged with him, at him, mocking and pointing all the while. It was the thing . . .

There had been a tree house, of that he was certain. A tree house with two rooms and half a roof. A boy could camp there at night, inside, yet staring up at the stars, exposed and yet safe. Alive and protected, he remembered what it was to be a boy. You could look at the motions of the sky and stars, enthralled at the wonder of life.

The wonder of life.

And that made him laugh; laugh like he had never laughed, and out loud—finally out loud—a laugh he had not known in so long that it defied recollection. Roaring with it, forgetting his place, the place. The others just walked away, knowing, deep down hating, what they saw. Back and forth on the concrete, rolling with the laughter, howling bursts that would not stop. The comedy of the thought bellowed through him until he no longer laughed or chuckled, but simply cried.

Slowly it all turned to pain. It all turns to pain. He had violated the contract, gone into feeling and humanity; he was acting out, which demonstrated a personal vulnerability that was, simply, forbidden. The guards were forced to respond, forced to get up from their chairs to protect society from the so-called monster that they, in their carelessness, had forged.

After enough whacks from a billy club, anyone will stop crying.

They dragged him away, to another cell where everything was exactly the same. He would be playing the same games with the same cards in a month or two or five. He would be lost to it again, forgetting this loss of composure until someone used it as an excuse to pound out their own bitterness.

The others called him weak for letting it get to him. Yet, they secretly—always secretly—harbored their own unspeakable envies.

Honor Yard looks the same, and the clothes we wear are the same. It is still prison. But instead of subjecting ourselves to a culture of hate and despair, we try to make lives that are worth more than discarded tears.

KENNETH E. HARTMAN

WHAT IS AND WHAT SHOULD BE

THE TENSION cuts through your clothes and into your skin like a jagged shank. Another alarm goes off, its pitched wailing, yelling out: there's trouble over here, be careful, be concerned, stay vigilant. The prisoners, all knotted up into little groups defined by skin color and tattoos, warily circle before sitting down. Each group watches the others closely. This could be a diversionary tactic to draw the guards off to a far corner of the compound to launch a sneak attack. The tower speaker is blaring a constant refrain, "Down on the yard, down on the yard."

The guards go running off to where a blue light is flashing. It could be anything from a false alarm to a full-on attempted takeover of the building or anything in between. Clubs drawn, pepper spray canisters in hand, they pour into the open doorway. On the yard, each group is sizing up its relative position. Because the alarms are essentially random, you never know where you might be when one goes off. It is a Russian roulette version of the chairs game. If the guards come out with combatants of different hues or conflicting tattoos you might get caught sitting on the ground, out of your seat, with your head kicked in. The longer it takes the guards to come back out, the sharper the tension gets. This happens multiple times every day. After a while, everyone is a raw nerve. The guards become so hyper-vigilant they react to everything with overwhelming force. The prisoners are so stressed they become landmines, tripwires extended out in every direction. Fear, masked as aggression, suppresses the higher modes of thought resulting in a defensive stance so rigid that all slights and perceived incursions provoke a mindless, out-of-proportion reaction. This goes on for years.

The breaks in this lunacy come in the form of periodic lock-downs that last for a day or a week or months, usually without any easily comprehended distinction. One stabbing could be a lockdown of a week, another a month. At first, the feeling on all sides is one of general relief. From having to watch hundreds of potential adversaries to only your cellmate is a diminution of stress by orders of magnitude. In those few cases when you are truly compatible with the man sharing your concrete box, the relaxation is invigorating. Normally, as the choice of who lives in your space is never truly voluntary, this is not the case. Now, whatever irritating peculiarities exist become heightened. Body odors and irrational hostilities come to the fore. It often devolves into a wary dance around hard-to-understand psychological problems and complex, deep-seated fears and resentments.

Regardless of compatibility, within a few days most prisoners begin to suffer an odd form of cabin fever, a depressive rage against the powerlessness of being trapped behind a steel door that only opens unpredictably and infrequently. Some men sleep all day, slipping into a self-induced semi-coma state of passive resistance. Others rev themselves up, adopting a maniacal workout routine consisting of hours and hours of furious grunting and sweating, as if by the force of transmitted kinetic energy the walls will spread apart. For many, the cabin fever expresses itself in the loss of rationality. This is particularly true for those with preexisting mental health problems, a startlingly large percentage of modern prisoners. For these unfortunates, the lockdown becomes too much to bear. Door kicking, random shouts, radios played at full volume for days on end, stopping up toilets to flood the tiers, and other similarly irrational behaviors proliferate throughout the buildings. Like a virulent, highly contagious disease, once a few men slip the constraints of civilized behavior, a general disorder is unleashed. Cell fights start to occur more frequently because there is no other way to escape intolerable situations. Asking for a move is tantamount to being an informer in the bizarro world of prison. Even if you do, the guards normal response is "show us some blood." Suicide attempts increase during these periods. The cell starts to shrink down on some prisoners until it is little more than a concrete coffin, squeezing out the desire to continue. In most prisons, a man spends more of his time on lockdown than off. This goes on for years.

The yards are peppered with these guys, these so-called "shotcallers." They are the ones who have become prison. Beyond the electrified fences, there is no existence for them besides that of scorned outcast. Faces tattooed with hideous and outrageous statements of ignorant rejectionism, they appear to rule this world by a sleight of hand so deftly performed few ever manage to perceive it. They receive special treatment, hold the best jobs, have the most movement around and between the buildings. Most ironically, in light of their complete disdain for the mores of the real world, they are accorded the most respect and humanity available from the guards.

It is to this group of thugs and psychopaths that the course of events on a prison yard is handed. To maintain their grip on power, held as it is without any justifiable claim, they must foment violence. Fear, as has been noted by dictators throughout history, is a powerful motivator of men. Follow our rules or you will be attacked, possibly killed. A whole series of dehumanizing and conforming policies are constantly pushed by their mercenaries, which only add to the stress and misery of this experience. You must wear your boots at all times because you must be prepared to fight for our group at all times. You must swear fealty to whichever bonehead happens to be the latest anointed holder of the keys to the yard. (Leaden irony in the use of "keys" to connote power to a prisoner, without actual keys, in a prison.) You must be willing to sacrifice your own good judgment to the lowest common denominator of herd thinking driven by the basest of human instincts. Worse, all of this will be actively supported by the guards empowering the shotcallers. Violence will be used, and encouraged, to achieve complete compliance. All will be penalized for the actions of the dumbest as if all were complicit. Refusal of an individual to play along will result in extremely negative consequences. This is the norm, the status quo. This goes on for years.

Idle hands are never a good thing. Combined with too often addled minds and tormented hearts, the results are disastrous. Of course, the kinds of programs needed to combat the outcome of lifetimes misspent and mismanaged are well known. Real and comprehensive substance abuse treatment, substantial education, mental health treatment, welcoming visitation, religious programming, creative outlets like art therapy, and regular and predictable recreation. All of these are proven to make a positive difference in the success or failure of prisoners. The problem is, heedless to reality, none of these are available to the average man. What substance abuse treatment there is provided boils down to hectoring and spotty enforcement, devoid of any actual treatment. Education in prison is little more than watching movies, doing crossword puzzles, and marking time in an overcrowded, loud little room monitored by a bored teacher marking his time until retirement. Mental health treatment is the issuance of pills to mask the unpleasant outward manifestations of madness and the generation of reams of paper to paint a picture of activity that does not exist beyond the motions, little of substance ever occurring. Visiting is the opposite of welcoming, being rather an effective bar to families and friends who are forced to endure a series of humiliations both petty and profound for making the obviously poor choice of consorting with prisoners. Beyond the highest hurdle, the location of prisons far from the places most prisoners originate, there is the maze of inconsistently applied rules visitors are forced to navigate. Those who lead religious programs and art therapies are both tossed into the same category of "inmate lover," which serves to both denigrate and accuse in one phrase. The prevailing opinion of those who guard prisons is that anyone who comes in to work with us must be dirty, somehow. As for regular and predictable recreation, the only constant in prison is its unpredictable and irregular nature. Each day has the quality of a crapshoot existence where the doors open with a capriciousness not unlike the weather in the mountains. Guards and administrators, teachers and doctors, who hold a fundamental belief in the futility of their mission, in the great waste of time it is to try and make a difference, manage these "programs." Lockdowns break up the continuity of any program, and lockdowns dominate the life of a prison. The result is tens of thousands of prisoners with nothing to do even remotely productive in nature. This goes on for years.

Corruption and incompetence hide behind chaos. This is the iron law of this particular jungle. Because the people who are charged with implementing the programs do not believe the programs have any chance of success, and because too many of those same people lack the requisite skills and education to effectively implement the programs in the first place, the maintenance of the state of chaos that rules prisons is in their best interest. It is the perfect dodge to responsibility: We would run these rehabilitative programs, but the inmates just won't cooperate. The gangs destroy anything good we try to do. The inmates are not capable of anything positive. These are the well-rehearsed excuses that play well to a public conditioned to assume that prisoners are, in fact, irredeemably recalcitrant, gang members who live to sow destruction and are all, simply, bad. To speak the truth, that most who run these institutions have little interest in our success, and a personal interest in our failure, is just not done. Nevertheless, to those of us who have spent enough time inside and struggled to achieve a level of consciousness beyond the walls, it is self-evident, this foul truth.

It is a question of economics. The fewer of us, the smaller the empire. It is a question of disposition. The system, in obeisance to the all-powerful god of security, trains its minions to consider prisoners as little more than security risks with legs. It is a question, most fundamentally, of ideology. They cannot, at the risk of professional suicide, accept that prisoners are capable of real and sustained growth. To abandon the company line of presumed failure would call into question the foundational elements underpinning this world. This world of humiliation and degradation, of isolation and stigma, would fall apart without the regular injection of negative poison that is the gasoline on the funeral pyres of so many wasted lives— lives on both sides of the fences.

Chaos is created with the unconscious cooperation of prisoners who desperately want to be part of something, even if that something is a system that feeds off our own suffering. The drug dealers and shotcallers are supported, years are spent in crushing lockdowns, violence is perpetuated, and those programs that could ameliorate the effects of tragic lives are suppressed or dismissed or subsumed in the terrible reality of prison. This chaos acts as a superbly effective smokescreen, a perfect blind behind which failure's familiars hide.

Even so, to be fair to those human beings that manage these places, the majority are not evil. They are rather, mostly, functionaries not capable of breaking out of the small box of prison thinking. Ideas like rehabilitation and reform bounce off of them as they search for the appropriate box to check on the appropriate form. The forms have no check boxes for abstractions like harm reduction or making a positive difference. It's all about restrictions and negative reinforcement: took this, took that, will take more if this and that don't result in compliance. People who missed first-year psychology must have designed the forms. They are all punishment and no reward. They are the products of reactive and punitive thinking that has never worked. These bureaucratic marionettes are simply not adept at reflection or analysis. Follow the form, go through the motions; any creative thinking will be punished. When the boxes are all checked off, and your ass is sufficiently covered by the appropriate ass-covering form, you have performed your duty. That the result of this is all too often, all too predictably, more failure, more violence and more chaos, is warped proof of the futility of this world. This has gone on for far too many years.

Deeply ensconced at all levels of the system is a much smaller group who actively work to defend the status quo, who consciously fight against positive change. These are the bullies who see their positions as opportunities to right the wrongs of their personal lives, the slights and injustices of high school still sharp in their memories. These are the crime victims who seek a place on this side of the fences to exact revenge, to take a bite out of criminals. And the ideologues, the most dangerous among the corrupt minority, the religious and political zealots who act with their own distorted sense of moral certitude. These are the creators of the forms that demand compliance to a failed system, a system that creates the failure it profits from, that it depends upon for its survival. These are the naysayers and the underminers, the hearts and brains of the current system. This has gone on for years, for decades and, absent radical change, it will go on forever.

All of this could lead an average person to conclude there is little hope for change, a not unreasonable conclusion. There is within the system this dejected sensibility; it's what ultimately drives off most reformers. But among prisoners, in particular those of us serving life sentences, there exists a stubborn strain of determination rooted in outrage that things have deteriorated to such an abysmal state. We know prison does not have to be this horrible. Prisoners do not need to be brutalized and traumatized at the hands of the system or their fellow prisoners. We know there are prison systems in this country that achieve markedly better results while treating their prisoners with much more humanity. We know the culture of gangs and violence, racism and self-destruction, is not a given. We also know that the groups in positions of power and influence have a personal stake in maintaining the status quo of failure, on both sides of the prisoner-guard divide. The strange twist of this is we lifers, who will be around for the long haul and who must see this world as our home, may be the only large group, the only long-term stakeholders, willing to fight for lasting change and endure the consequences for mounting the challenge.

It was in this vein of thinking that a small group of us got together and came up with a plan to create a transformational yard in one of the most dysfunctional of California's prisons. We had all watched as the creeping maelstrom of systemic disorder invaded our corner of the system. In the space of a few years, the whole prison was engulfed in massive race riots, organized attacks on guards, retaliatory brutality against prisoners, and a stunning level of corruption camouflaged in the tear gas laced clouds of chaos. It was never a good place, but now it became a terrible, frightening and dangerous place. This was the time of the final ascendancy of gangs to power throughout the system, including prison guard gangs in the worst of the prisons. It appeared that those who knew better, the old veteran guards who came from before the era of outright inmate hating, left and turned over the reins to the new thugs in uniforms. And these new thugs, empowered by the victims' rights movement's incessant demands for ever more punishment and the pandering of opportunistic politicians, launched a war on prisoners. The ruse was that by taking everything away from us that made existence inside tolerable, it would make prison so intolerable an experience it would drive us into compliance and terrify us into never coming back. We all knew, on both sides of the fence and with complete certainty, the result would be disaster.

As the disaster unfolded, we came up with a proposal to create one yard for those prisoners who wanted to stay out of the whirlpool sucking us all down. I couched it in language that appealed to the demand for genuflection before the security altar and the basic need to have the necessary services (food preparation, laundry, and the like) performed by prisoners not nursing wounds incurred in the latest riot. We had the great good fortune of one of the last wardens to come up through the non-custody ranks (he had been a teacher) and a few smart and humane staff willing to carry the water for the project. The waves of tragedies that had scoured this prison left everyone not interested in the triumph of chaos open to experimentation.

The specifics were simple: take only those prisoners who volunteered, who had a record of positive behavior, and enact a strict system to disempower the worst elements of our own ranks. This would be a yard devoid of drug dealers, devoid of shotcallers, and devoid of all the chaos these groups bring with them. Anyone who broke the rules would be removed back to the hell of the other yards, a powerful and visible disincentive. Additionally, and most controversially as it turned out, positive incentives for successful participation would be included—a few modest carrots to balance out the thicket of sticks.

The warden ordered implementation and the process was completed in a few months. The recalcitrant prisoners left of their own accord, taking with them the drugs and violence and the grossest of stupidity. Within a six-month period, a yard with a housing unit once known to all as "Thunder Dome" was fully functional. Gone were the negative elements that destroy prisoners' ability and will to achieve the kind of transformation necessary to successful reintegration back into free society. The madness of constant alarms interrupting the flow of every day simply stopped. Lockdowns ceased for years, literally. The shotcallers, having no shots to call, disappeared, melting back into the torment from which they emanated. And programs proliferated, exploding in a great blast of pent-up demand to be a part of something, anything worthwhile.

In the next few years, something wholly unexpected was achieved on this yard known as the "Honor Program." It was far beyond the peace and positive energy that replaced the fearful tension, beyond the absence of lockdowns and alarms and casualties, beyond even the programs self-initiated by prisoners proving many of us actually desire to do good. What happened was the emergence of a movement that grew out beyond the fence line. At first, mostly our families and friends—which is to be expected—but then political figures, community leaders and local nonprofits got involved. Men on the yard started to write the newspapers, describing something incongruous, practically unbelievable out of one of these places. Good things were happening on a prison yard deep in the mire of what is, arguably, the worst prison system in the country. Television crews came in to document this strange aberration. Leaders of the state government showed up to witness how good could possibly have taken seed in such barren soil. It was a heady time. For a little while, many of us believed we had crossed the Rubicon, or rather we had pulled the prison across; there would be no turning back to the beforetime of such obvious failure and waste.

During the few years things reached their apogee, the transformation was complete and deep. We organized our own sports leagues and required all teams to be integrated of our own accord. This is such a revolutionary act in the hyper-racialized world of California prisons that administrators from other prisons came in to see it for themselves. "How did you do this?" one of them asked me, a look of utter astonishment on his face. We recruited the educated from amongst our own ranks and set up formal instruction in an empty classroom. Foreign languages, mathematics, creative writing and business courses took off with diverse and peaceful groups of students eager to learn. The best artists formed a collective to donate their work to local charities. A prisoner group formed to counsel at-risk youth, gaining widespread recognition. Men conducted their own religious services, without any troubles. (Before the implementation of the Honor Program, when the chapel required a staff presence for any activity to take place, the area was the site of endless fighting and rampant drug dealing.) At one point, there were real plans to bring in service dogs for us to train. Prisoners performing an indisputably valuable function for the community. It was a moment of genuine pride for all of us who had labored to make this happen, prisoners and our supporters, and those staff who had the courage to break out of the negative expectation.

Then, something else unexpected happened. In retrospect, it is obvious why it happened, but this was during our moment of greatest success. We were blinded in the footlights, unaccustomed warmth. We didn't see it coming. The elements that stand behind their barricade of disorder launched a concerted effort to undo all that we had done. The manufactured need for ever-increasing security, which means more positions and more money, was being exposed by our peaceful yard. Talk was beginning to spread up and down the dark empire of opening more yards like this one, of injecting the system with an inoculation of positive energy. Without the cover story of prisoners as unmanageable beasts, the more uncomfortable truth might be exposed. Even though a growing body of scholarship and a towering pile of studies and reports documented the mismanagement and incompetence at the heart of the prison system's failure, the sad facts on the ground stymied efforts to bring about change. This was the strategy, and it had always worked to wear out the reformers, something it continues to accomplish. The public's desire to see prisoners treated humanely is shallow, at best. Added to this the constant, well-funded drumbeat of demands for revenge dressed up in justice's flowing robes, which keeps the focus on punishment for the sake of the infliction of pain. The reformers know this only results in further victimization and further vast sums of scarce dollars poured down the drain of prisons. The trouble is, the bullies know they can count on some twisted wreck of a human spat out to the real world, after years of neglect and torment, committing a senseless and atrocious act. The calls for justice (punishment and pain) shout down the appeals to reason, and the circus of horrors then resumes, unmoved and unchanged.

We brought it on ourselves, to a certain degree. Perhaps if we had been silent, had quietly enjoyed our little space of peace, the reaction would not have come. But we couldn't. We had proven it was not necessary to exist as animals, and we wanted to share this revelation for the benefit of the many thousands trapped in the quagmire elsewhere. The truth is we felt like we had done something demonstrably good. For men whose lives have been defined by everything but good, the desire to take ownership of good is powerful. This last impulse, this claiming to us what was rightfully ours, turned out to be another irritant of considerable weight. Even some of the more progressive staff, who seemed to appreciate the positive direction events had taken, could not accept that the bulk of the changes were on account of us—that our efforts, primarily, had resulted in this good turn. They were offended, their feelings hurt, perhaps. But the department's administrators were livid at our audacity. How could prisoners have done anything good? This was an outrageous usurpation. If anything good had happened, which they mostly now insisted had not, it was solely on account of their decisions and their superior knowledge. In the final analysis, the Honor Program was denigrated as little more than mollycoddling, at best, and perhaps nothing more than a sham behind which a slew of gang-banging, drug dealing regular (read bad) inmates were hiding.

Once the gloves came off, and with a resounding slap on the concrete table they did come off, the next few years devolved into a series of political battles between the movement we created and led, and the big bosses in the state capitol. Reports favoring the program aired on television and appeared in print. A bill passed in the state legislature that would have mandated the program only to be vetoed by the governor at the insistence of the department. All the while, as we did all we could to hold our place, the undermining went on. The best staff, the ones who had been willing to support this better way, were transferred or otherwise penalized. The standards we had set up to create a workable population were deliberately ignored as the yard collapsed closer to the violence and degeneracy of a normal yard.

The past couple of years we have spent coming on to half our time on lockdown, although, thus far, the issues have been manufactured. We still have held off the worst of our own idiocy, though it grows stronger every day. The yard is now three distinct groups: we who started this and struggle to keep it alive, a growing group of blockheads and tattooed faces who work mindlessly to end it, and a final group of mental health cases who wander around like human I.E.D.'s waiting to explode at the most inconvenient of moments. It is a true shame, and it is very deliberate and purposeful what has been done.

Regardless of the ultimate fate of this particular corner of the concrete and razor wire empire, whether we are able to pull yet another rabbit out of our state-issued hats and stave off the end, we proved that prison doesn't need to be the wasteful, destructive monstrosity it has become. It is not a foregone conclusion that prisoners must descend into tribal primitivism and atavistic violence. We also proved that most prisoners want to be productive, contributing members of society. If only the impotent rage against the daily degradations of prison life can be lessened by the creation of a semblance of peace and respect, the average prisoner can focus on recreating himself, on disabusing his previously held notions of who or what he is supposed to be. We proved this life does not necessarily need to be a pointless, meaningless experience in futility.

What with all the millions of words spewed and the boatloads of ink splattered on forests of paper seeking to convince the average citizen of the great waste of time it is to seek rehabilitation, and the far greater need to exact many pounds of flesh, a logical response to all of this is, Why should I care? The simple answer is found at the front gate of every prison in the form of the angry mass of ill-clothed, destitute men pouring out every day. Men who have lived a Hobbesian nightmare without a moment's break. No substance abuse treatment, no mental health care, no education of any kind, and no meaningful attachments in the communities to which they are headed, which all translates to without any real hope of success. These men will be your neighbors. These men, out of an endless battlefield of shame and rage, will be walking down your streets.

Contrast that daily dose of poison with a man who has lived a life of peaceful reflection and service, who has been able to receive the treatments and skills needed to reenter the community prepared to participate. It is not a question of whether this man deserved to be helped or not—it is a question of societal self-interest. Building up the fallen is worthy even beyond the ethical issues of a just society. It is worthy from the pragmatic perspective of the American sense of doing what works because it works, because it achieves the results we all want to achieve. No matter how emotionally satisfying it may be to pursue the twisted ideal of revenge, in practice what falls off that dead tree is indigestible. To quote the maxim of the moment, the approach needs to be smart on crime. The smartest thing is to apprehend the offender, seek a just and appropriate penalty, and then set to work making the chance for rehabilitation more than a slogan or a mirage obscured by the glare of idiotic policies. The program we created, that we have fought the good fight for, is that real chance.

We have, finally, proven another fact of this world. It is a terrible fact that ought to engender a great uprising of disgust and outcries for immediate reform. The people who manage the prison system, largely, have no desire to rehabilitate prisoners. Worse, they see rehabilitation as a threat to their livelihoods. All the pious talk of protecting the public and salving the wounds of crime victims is nothing more than public relations spin. The experience of this program's fight for survival is stark testimony to this truth that needs no embellishment. If change is going to come—and come it most certainly must— this truth needs to be addressed, first.